OECD-FAO Business Handbook on Deforestation and Due Diligence in Agricultural Supply Chains

Please cite this publication as:
OECD/FAO (2023), *OECD-FAO Business Handbook on Deforestation and Due Diligence in Agricultural Supply Chains*, OECD Publishing, Paris, https://doi.org/10.1787/c0d4bca7-en.

ISBN 978-92-64-72532-4 (print)
ISBN 978-92-64-51308-2 (pdf)
ISBN 978-92-64-99794-3 (HTML)
ISBN 978-92-64-79712-3 (epub)

FAO:
ISBN 978-92-5-137953-0 (print and pdf)

Photo credits: cover © STILLFX/Getty Images.

Corrigenda to OECD publications may be found on line at: www.oecd.org/about/publishing/corrigenda.htm.

Foreword

This *OECD-FAO Business Handbook on Deforestation and Due Diligence in Agricultural Supply Chains* (Handbook) aims to help companies embed considerations on deforestation and forest degradation in corporate due diligence procedures. It is based on the risk-based due diligence framework set out in the *OECD-FAO Guidance for Responsible Agricultural Supply Chains* (OECD-FAO Guidance) and the *OECD Due Diligence Guidance for Responsible Business Conduct*.

This Handbook forms part of the OECD and FAO's work associated with the OECD-FAO Guidance for Responsible Agricultural Supply Chains (OECD-FAO Guidance) (OECD-FAO, 2016[1]) and Responsible Business Conduct (RBC) in Agriculture.

The sourcing and trade of many agricultural commodities involves a complex network of business relationships, including producers, farmers, traders, suppliers and other actors that are part of global agrifood supply chains. As global demand for food grows, challenges can arise which may result in adverse impacts related to agricultural expansion, including into forests and other natural ecosystems. As a result, business decisions made by companies sourcing, processing and selling agricultural commodities and products can cause, contribute to or be directly linked to deforestation or forest degradation.

For almost 15 years, companies and stakeholders in the timber sector have widely applied due diligence approaches in response to regulations (e.g. the European Union Timber Regulation and the United States of America Lacey Act (Lacey, 2008[2]) aimed at ensuring the legal origin of timber. To facilitate due diligence and reduce risks, timber exporting countries have developed verification or assurance systems to prove and document the legality, sustainability and traceability of wood products. In parallel, the UN and the OECD have developed recommendations and guidelines on how companies can integrate risk-based due diligence in their business decisions and business relationships to identify and address supply chain risks which have an impact on people and the planet. These efforts have resulted in work on reducing environmental and social risks among agrifood enterprises, in co-operation with stakeholders from farmer organisations, civil society and enterprises themselves. However, many enterprises still struggle to understand how the risks of deforestation and forest degradation can manifest in their supply chains and how they as enterprises can take practical measures to identify, prevent and address these risks through risk-based due diligence.

This Handbook aims to help business address deforestation and forest degradation risks in global agricultural supply chains through risk-based due diligence, including by integrating existing business efforts to trace timber legality, where relevant. The Handbook is designed for agrifood enterprises that source or use commodities and products that may be associated with deforestation or forest degradation. While impacts on forests occur upstream in the supply chain, companies downstream often drive the demand for these commodities, which in turn increases deforestation risks. This Handbook has thus been designed for use by enterprises along the entire supply chain, from production to retail.

As part of the development of this Handbook, the OECD and FAO convened a Multi-Stakeholder Expert Working Group (MSWG) comprised of stakeholders from business, government, civil society, academia and others to support the drafting of this Handbook, including elements and types of information that would be useful to help companies operationalise risk-based due diligence to address deforestation. In addition to feedback from the MSWG, an informal public consultation was organised from June to July 2022.

Acknowledgements

The OECD and FAO would like to thank all stakeholders who contributed to the development of this Handbook, ranging from enterprises, academia, civil society organisations and certification bodies to numerous governments from around the world. Particular thanks go to independent expert Duncan Brack who led the drafting process of this Handbook in co-operation with the OECD and FAO and the Multi-Stakeholder Working Group (MSWG).

At the OECD Centre for Responsible Business Conduct (OECD RBC Centre), the Handbook was drafted and supervised by Shivani Kannabhiran, Sophia Gnych and Sebastian Weber. The OECD would like to further thank the Working Parties on Responsible Business Conduct (WPRBC) and Agricultural Policies and Markets (APM) for contributing inputs and comments to this Handbook.

At the Food and Agriculture Organization of the United Nations (FAO), the Handbook was drafted by Tomislav Ivančić, Caroline Merle and Kristin DeValue, under the supervision of Pascal Liu, Tiina Vähänen and Serena Fortuna. Special acknowledgment goes to Astrid Agostini, as well as to colleagues in FAO's Forestry and Markets and Trade Divisions, and offices around the world who provided technical support to this Handbook.

This handbook is funded by the German Federal Ministry for Economic Cooperation and Development (BMZ) and supported by the Deutsche Gesellschaft für Internationale Zusammenarbeit (GIZ) GmbH. Franziska Rau, Advisor at the Initiative for Sustainable Agricultural Supply Chains (INA), GIZ, provided valuable input to the Handbook on behalf of the INA deforestation team.

Table of contents

FIGURES

TABLES

Follow OECD Publications on:

https://twitter.com/OECD

https://www.facebook.com/theOECD

https://www.linkedin.com/company/organisation-eco-cooperation-development-organisation-cooperation-developpement-eco/

https://www.youtube.com/user/OECDiLibrary

https://www.oecd.org/newsletters/

Follow FAO on:

Food and Agriculture Organization of the United Nations

https://twitter.com/FAOSocioEcon
https://twitter.com/faostatistics
https://twitter.com/FAOKnowledge

https://www.facebook.com/UNFAO

https://www.linkedin.com/company/fao

https://www.youtube.com/user/FAOoftheUN

https://instagram.com/fao

Executive summary

The OECD-FAO Guidance for Responsible Agricultural Supply Chains (OECD-FAO Guidance) helps enterprises in the agricultural sector observe existing international standards for responsible business conduct in agricultural supply chains. The OECD-FAO Guidance is an example of the growing recognition of how risk-based due diligence can help enterprises identify and respond to risks in their operations and global supply chains. In addition to due diligence actions taken by enterprises, several governments have adopted or plan to introduce, mandatory obligations of due diligence in global supply chains, including to address deforestation concerns.

Business decisions made by companies sourcing, processing and selling agricultural commodities or food products may have an impact on forests, which can include deforestation. As a salient risk related to sourcing, deforestation can also have larger impacts on ecosystems and the people depending on them. However, many enterprises struggle to understand how risks of deforestation and forest degradation can manifest in their supply chains, including on practical measures they can take to identify, prevent and address these risks through risk-based due diligence.

This Handbook was developed by OECD and FAO to help companies embed considerations on deforestation and forest degradation into their responsible sourcing and corporate due diligence efforts. It is informed by FAO's extensive work and experience on halting deforestation and forest degradation and promoting responsible governance of tenure. The handbook builds on the leading international, government-backed standards on supply chain due diligence and responsible business conduct: the OECD Guidelines for Multinational Enterprises on Responsible Business Conduct and the associated due diligence framework introduced in the OECD-FAO Guidance for Responsible Agricultural Supply Chains and the OECD Due Diligence Guidance for Responsible Business Conduct. This Handbook demonstrates how the OECD-FAO Guidance can be applied to address deforestation by contextualising existing recommendations and helping users understand how to proactively introduce due diligence and reduce the potential risk of deforestation taking place in their supply chains.

Introduction

This chapter introduces the Handbook, outlines who it has been developed for and provides key definitions.

This *OECD-FAO Business Handbook on Deforestation and Due Diligence in Agricultural Supply Chains* (Handbook) aims to help companies embed considerations on deforestation and forest degradation in corporate due diligence procedures. It builds on the risk-based due diligence framework set out in the OECD-FAO Guidance and the OECD Due Diligence Guidance for Responsible Business Conduct.

The Handbook provides background information, resources and practical actions that enterprises can take when implementing each of the steps of risk-based due diligence in line with the OECD-FAO Guidance. It draws on current corporate practice, including existing tools and resources, data and metrics that are available to support enterprises when they consider how best to identify and avoid deforestation and forest degradation.

Key definitions

Deforestation: The FAO defines deforestation as the conversion of forest to other land use independently whether human-induced or not (FAO, 2020[3]).

Forest degradation: There is no FAO or other standard definition for forest degradation; the FAO encourages countries to define it themselves. The definition included in the Accountability Framework proposed by a group of international NGOs, which applies to other natural ecosystems as well as forests, is: "Changes within a natural ecosystem that significantly and negatively affect its species composition, structure, and/or function and reduce the ecosystem's capacity to supply products, support biodiversity, and/or deliver ecosystem services" (Accountability Framework, 2020[4]).

For a full list of definitions, see the Glossary.

Who is this Handbook for?

The Handbook is designed for enterprises in agrifood supply chains which source or use commodities and products that may be associated with deforestation or forest degradation. While the Handbook is primarily concerned with the impacts of land use, planting and harvesting on forests, it can be used by enterprises along the entire supply chain, from production to retail.

Increasingly, companies are introducing risk-based due diligence approaches in their policies and procedures to help guide their responsible sourcing efforts and promote responsible business conduct. Many small- and medium-sized enterprises (SMEs) struggle to address trade and market requirements linked to responsible business conduct, including deforestation. To help smaller enterprises address deforestation, each chapter of this Handbook features a box with suggestions on how SMEs can introduce risk-based due diligence in line with the OECD-FAO Guidance.

The Handbook can also be a resource for financial institutions as they assess and evaluate potential business partners' policies and activities relevant to due diligence expectations and potential deforestation. Annex A of the Handbook lists resources related to deforestation.

Forests, natural ecosystems and conversion

The due diligence framework described in this Handbook applies both to deforestation and forest degradation. For ease of reading, the term 'deforestation' is here used to apply to both.

Forests are not the only natural ecosystem that may be adversely affected by conversion to agricultural production. Savannah, grasslands, peatlands and wetlands, among others, can also be at risk when considering land use. Many due diligence policies adopted by enterprises now cover the conversion of these ecosystems alongside forests, and incorporate references to, for example, the protection of high conservation value and high carbon stock areas. While this Handbook focuses only on forests, the due diligence steps it describes are generally also applicable to the conversion of other natural ecosystems.

A full list of definitions used in this Handbook is included in the Glossary.

Forests and deforestation

This chapter introduces deforestation and forest degradation in the context of global supply chains. It presents the magnitude of the problem and its origins in commodity production and sourcing, along with the development challenges that can contribute to deforestation in different contexts.

Healthy forests are vital to the three pillars of sustainable development: economic, social and environmental. Continued business growth and jobs in the agricultural sector, and global food security, depend on forests. Forest ecosystems are the largest terrestrial carbon sink, critical to meeting climate goals; they also regulate rainfall and water cycles and help to maintain stable local environments, which are essential to supporting livelihoods and sustainable agricultural production. Approximately 1.6 billion people depend on forests for their livelihood, including about 70 million Indigenous Peoples. Forests contain more than 60 000 different tree species and provide habitats for a large majority of animal species. (FAO, 2020[3]; FAO and UNEP, 2020[5]).

In 2020, 31% of the world's land area – 4 billion hectares – was covered by forest. Since 1990 an estimated 420 million hectares of forests have been lost through deforestation (FAO, 2020[3]). From 2015 to 2020, the rate of deforestation was estimated at 10 million hectares per year, though afforestation and reforestation has supported forest recovery in some parts of the world (FAO, 2020[3]). Loss of forests, particularly natural forest, was especially high in the tropics over this period (see Figure 1).

Forest degradation is a result of unsustainable logging operations, wood fuel extraction, shifting agriculture, grazing or fires and affects forest ecosystems in tropical, temperate and boreal biomes alike. In all these cases the forest retains the capacity to regrow, but these activities typically reduce forest cover faster than it naturally recovers and affect the diversity of species hosted in those forests (FAO and UNEP, 2020[5]). While forest degradation is difficult to measure, studies suggest that it accounts for about one-third of the overall impact of tree cover loss, measured in terms of carbon emissions (Federici, 2015[6]).

Figure 1. Deforestation, 2000-2018

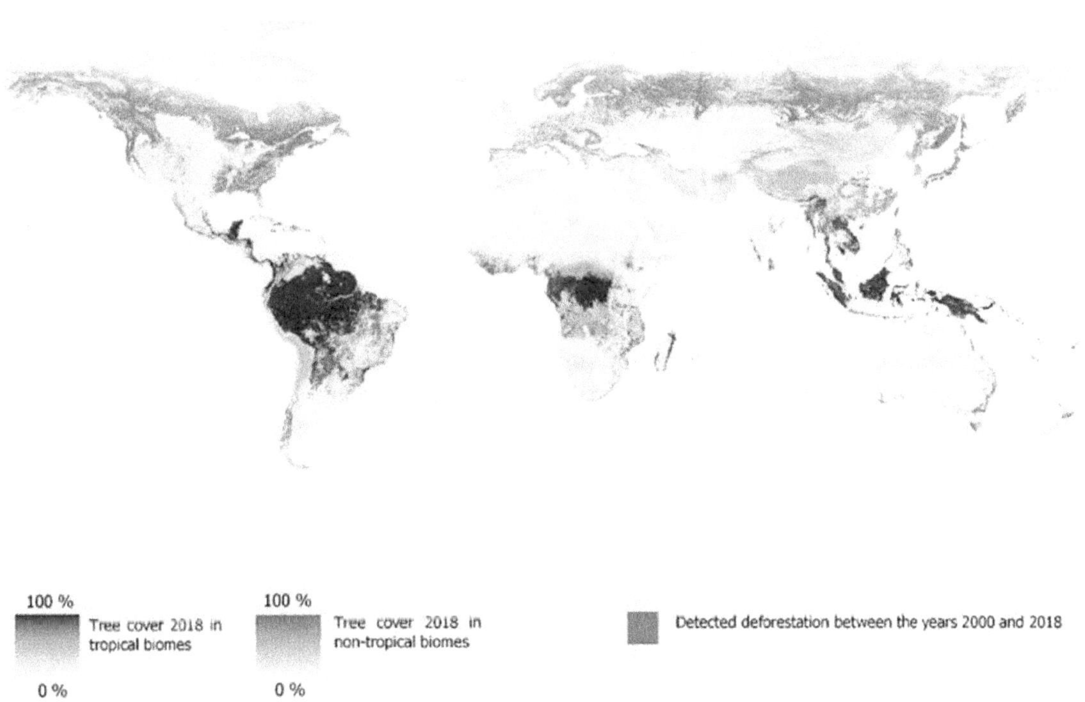

Source: FAO (2022[7]), FRA 2020 Remote Sensing Survey, https://www.fao.org/forest-resources-assessment/remote-sensing/fra-2020-remote-sensing-survey/en/

Impacts of agricultural production on forests

Agricultural production can both drive deforestation and be negatively impacted by deforestation. FAO's global Remote Sensing Survey of forest resources estimates that from 2000-18 nearly 90% of global deforestation was a result of agricultural expansion, including 52% from cropland expansion and 38% from livestock grazing (FAO, 2021[8]). Figure 2 illustrates the main drivers of deforestation by region. Similarly, deforestation, coupled with climate change, can also greatly impact agricultural production, which can in turn have significant impacts on food availability and demand.[1]

Figure 2. Main deforestation drivers across the world's regions

Drivers of deforestation by region, 2000-18 (in Mha)

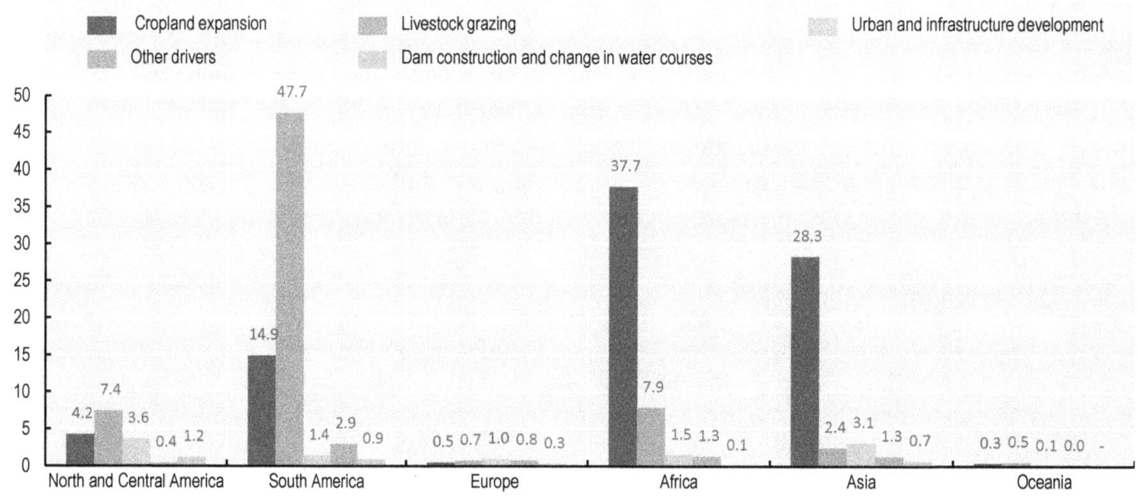

Source: FAO (2022[7]), FRA 2020 Remote Sensing Survey, https://www.fao.org/forest-resources-assessment/remote-sensing/fra-2020-remote-sensing-survey/en/

A range of factors underpin the link between deforestation and agricultural production (Geist, 2002[9]). While growth and development have raised millions out of poverty, they have also increased demand for food and led to changes in lifestyles and diets as people consume lower volumes of staple foods and more meat, dairy products, fruit and vegetables, and processed foods. These trends are projected to continue (OECD-FAO, 2021[10]) as the global population is anticipated to reach 9.7 billion people by 2050 (UN, 2019[11]). Taking dietary changes and other factors into account, this implies a growth in food demand of 35-56% (Van Dijk, 2021[12]), potentially increasing demand for land and pressure on forests.

The liberalisation of trade and business has encouraged the growth of global supply chains; an estimated one-third of agri-food exports are now traded within global value chains (FAO, 2022[13]). While the act of deforestation takes place at specific locations upstream in the supply chain, downstream firms and suppliers play a critical role in ensuring that the risk of deforestation is addressed within the commodity supply chains from which they source.

It should be noted that a significant proportion of the clearance of forests for agriculture has been illegal. A comprehensive survey published in 2021 estimated that 69% of the conversion of tropical forests for agriculture that had taken place between 2013 and 2019 had been conducted in violation of national laws and regulations (Forest Trends, 2021[14]). Illegal logging (for timber) remains a serious concern in many countries, with an estimated value in international trade at between USD 50-150 billion a year (World Bank, 2019[15]).

Agricultural commodities and deforestation

Based on studies of the drivers discussed above, deforestation linked to agriculture has often been associated with a select group of commodities (Pendrill, 2019[16]). However, business, demand and trade can oscillate over time. Neither supply nor demand is fixed, and growth in demand for new agricultural products can drive deforestation in other contexts, including in temperate climates.

International attention is commonly given to the impacts on forests of certain commodities which have seen increased production and export over recent decades, often dependent on expanding land for agricultural use by reducing forest cover. Commodities cultivated or grown in an area after it is deforested are considered as "direct drivers" of deforestation. It is the manner in which these commodities are produced, not the commodities themselves, however, that links them to deforestation.

A small group of commodities have received wider attention because recently deforested lands are often used for their production. These include beef, dairy products and leather from cattle, soybeans, palm oil, cocoa, coffee, wood and rubber. Consequently, public and private responses and multi-stakeholder initiatives have tended to adopt commodity-specific approaches in their efforts towards more sustainable production models, respecting forests. Examples include the Amazon Soy Moratorium signed in 2006 where 90% of companies in the Brazilian soy market committed to avoiding the purchase of soy grown on recently deforested areas in the Brazilian Amazon. Likewise, the governments of Côte d'Ivoire and Ghana and 35 leading cocoa and chocolate companies have joined together in the Forest and Cocoa Initiative to eliminate cocoa related deforestation and restore forest areas.

Global initiatives on deforestation

Many efforts are being made to decouple commodity production from deforestation. While meeting international targets associated with deforestation, particularly those adopted before 2020 (see Table 1) have proved challenging, they have stimulated action by a wide range of companies producing, trading and using commodities associated with deforestation. Commitments to eliminate or reduce deforestation in corporate supply chains have become common in companies trading in and using timber, palm oil and cocoa; they are less common for other commodities. An analysis of 675 companies in 2021 disclosing forest risk in their supply chains to CDP found that 66% possessed a policy related to deforestation, while 38% had a general or commodity-specific company-wide no-deforestation / conversion policy (CDP/AFI, 2022[17]).

Table 1 provides examples of the wide range of international initiatives on deforestation associated with agricultural and timber supply chains since 2010;[2] these include initiatives such as soft law, SDGs, private sector initiatives, as well as multi-stakeholder initiatives.

Table 1. Examples of international initiatives on deforestation

Date	Organisation / Initiative	Commitments
2008 through 2015	UN Framework Convention on Climate Change – REDD, then REDD+, Framework	Guide activities in the forest sector that reduce emissions from deforestation and forest degradation, as well as the sustainable management of forests and the conservation and enhancement of forest carbon stocks in developing countries.
2010	Consumer Goods Forum (global industry network of retailers, manufacturers and service providers)	Zero net deforestation in membership's supply chains by 2020 in key commodities: soy, palm oil, timber / paper and pulp, beef.
2012	Tropical Forest Alliance (global partnership of governments, companies, civil society, Indigenous Peoples, local communities, UN agencies)	Reduction in tropical deforestation associated with the sourcing of commodities such as palm oil, soy, cattle products and paper and pulp. Promotes and supports

Date	Organisation / Initiative	Commitments
		regional multi-stakeholder initiatives.
2014	New York Declaration on Forests (signatories now include over 200 national and local governments, companies, and civil society, community and Indigenous Peoples' organisations)	At least halve the rate of loss of natural forests globally by 2020, strive to end natural forest loss by 2030; support private-sector goal of eliminating deforestation from production of agricultural commodities by no later than 2020; significantly reduce deforestation derived from other economic sectors by 2020.
2015	UN Sustainable Development Goals	SDG 15.2: "By 2020, promote the implementation of sustainable management of all types of forests, halt deforestation, restore degraded forests and substantially increase afforestation and reforestation globally." (Also SDG 12.6: "Encourage companies, especially large and transnational companies, to adopt sustainable practices and to integrate sustainability information into their reporting cycle.")
2020	Consumer Goods Forum Forest-Positive Coalition of Action	Coalition of major companies aiming to support deforestation- and conversion-free enterprises through multi-stakeholder, integrated land use initiatives in key production landscapes. Commodity-specific roadmaps for action for soy, palm oil, cattle and pulp and paper.
2021	Glasgow Leaders' Declaration on Forests and Land Use (signed by 141 countries at the 26th UN Climate Change Conference [COP26])	"Work collectively to halt and reverse forest loss and land degradation by 2030 while delivering sustainable development and promoting an inclusive rural transformation". Specific commitments include to: "facilitate trade and development policies, internationally and domestically, that promote sustainable development, and sustainable commodity production and consumption, that work to countries' mutual benefit, and that do not drive deforestation and land degradation".
2021	Forest, Agriculture and Commodity Trade (FACT) Dialogue Roadmap for Action (statement by 27 governments and EU (representing largest producers and consumers of internationally traded agricultural commodities) at COP26)	Aims to promote sustainable development and trade of agricultural commodities while protecting and sustainably managing forests and other critical ecosystems; Includes indicative actions on trade and market development; smallholder support; traceability and transparency; and research, development and innovation.

A number of consumer countries have seen the emergence of initiatives aimed at ensuring that the entire national market is supplied with certified sustainable commodities – particularly for palm oil and cocoa – by a target date; sometimes these voluntary initiatives include governments too. Similar alliances have developed in several producer countries, such as the Zero-Deforestation Agreement on Palm Oil in Colombia. A number of producer countries have also developed their own national standards and certification schemes for specific commodities; examples include the Indonesian and Malaysian Sustainable Palm Oil standards and the African Standard for Sustainable Cocoa.

Recent years have also seen the emergence and uptake of commodity-focused multi-stakeholder roundtables and engagement platforms for collective action – such as the Africa Sustainable Commodities Initiative – and voluntary sustainability standards and associated certification schemes (see Annex A). Several financial institutions have adopted commitments not to provide finance for activities associated with deforestation.[3]

Legislation on deforestation and risk-based due diligence

In response to rising concerns over climate change and deforestation, some governments are introducing obligations for enterprises to conduct due diligence to address a range of risks in their operations and supply chains, including deforestation. These obligations complement the initiatives mentioned above and include:

- General corporate obligations of due diligence, applying to an enterprise's entire operations and supply chains, not specific to any sector or product, and not linked to placing products on the market.
- Requirement for due diligence to be undertaken with regard to particular criteria (e.g. legal production, or zero-deforestation) before specified products can be placed on the market, imported or exported.

The implementation of risk-based due diligence as described in this Handbook, according to the OECD-FAO Guidance may support enterprises to meet such obligations.[4]

Due diligence in agricultural supply chains

This chapter introduces the overall concept of risk-based due diligence as set out by the OECD-FAO Guidance for Responsible Agricultural Supply Chains.

"Due diligence" is understood as the process through which enterprises identify, prevent, mitigate and account for how they address the actual and potential adverse impacts of their own operations, their supply chain and other business relationships. This is the approach to due diligence recommended by the *OECD-FAO Guidance for Responsible Agricultural Supply Chains* (OECD-FAO Guidance) and the cross-sectoral *Due Diligence Guidance for Responsible Business Conduct* (OECD, 2018, p. 15[18]). Due diligence in this context is thus an integral part of business decision-making and risk management. The due diligence framework of the OECD-FAO Guidance can be used by all enterprises operating along agricultural supply chains, from upstream production to downstream retail.

The OECD-FAO Guidance due diligence framework

The risk-based due diligence framework in the OECD-FAO Guidance describes the steps an enterprise can take to identify, prevent and address risks in their operations, supply chains and business relationships. Figure 3 illustrates the five-step process, as well as integrating the *Remediation of Adverse Impacts*, which forms a sixth step within the cross-sectoral Due Diligence Guidance for Responsible Business Conduct. The protection of forests and the avoidance of deforestation are mentioned on several occasions in the OECD-FAO Guidance but are not discussed in detail. As such, this Handbook supplements the OECD-FAO Guidance by using risk-based due diligence to identify and address deforestation risks in global agricultural supply chains.

Figure 3. The OECD-FAO Guidance due diligence framework

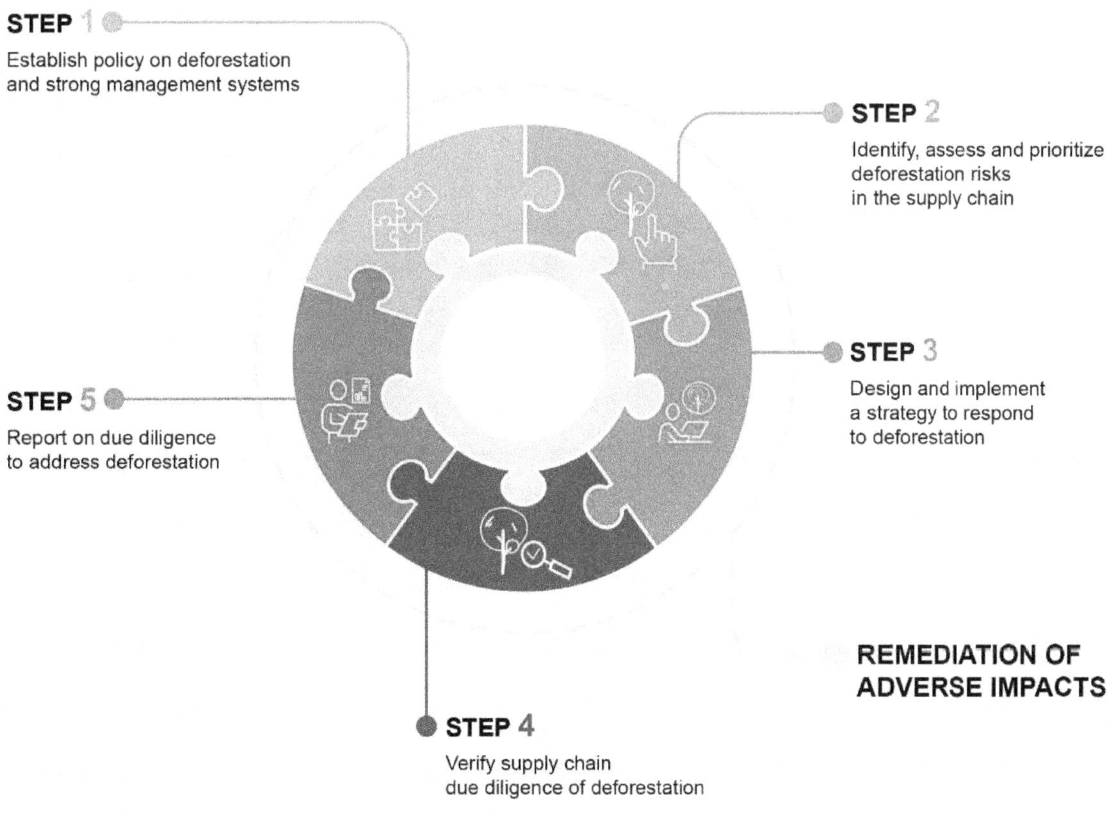

Source: Adapted from (OECD-FAO, 2016[1]) and the (OECD, 2018[18]).

What is meant by "risk" for due diligence

For many enterprises, the term "risk" means primarily risks to the enterprise – financial risk, market risk, operational risk, reputational risk, etc. In the field of responsible business conduct, risk refers to the severity and likelihood of adverse impacts on people, the environment and society that enterprises cause, contribute to, or to which they are directly linked through business operations and sourcing practices. In other words, it is an outward-facing approach to risk. It is important to note that there are many potential underlying drivers of deforestation. Factors such as poverty, human rights abuses, the rights, resources and capacities of local communities and Indigenous Peoples, the uncertain status of land and forest tenure rights, corruption and weaknesses in governance and law enforcement may all act as root causes for deforestation risks.

Defining the involvement of an enterprise with regard to adverse impacts

An enterprise can either cause adverse impacts, contribute to them, or be directly linked to them through its operations, products and services by a business relationship (see Figure 4). This understanding of the relationship of the enterprise to deforestation, or the risk of deforestation, is important, as it guides an enterprise on what it is expected to do in response to the impact. Depending on its relationship to the impact, taking action to respond to deforestation or deforestation risks could mean taking steps to directly remedy the impact, cease activities causing the impact or prevent the potential impact, or use leverage to influence the entity causing the impact.

Figure 4. Addressing adverse impacts based on examples of relationships to the impact

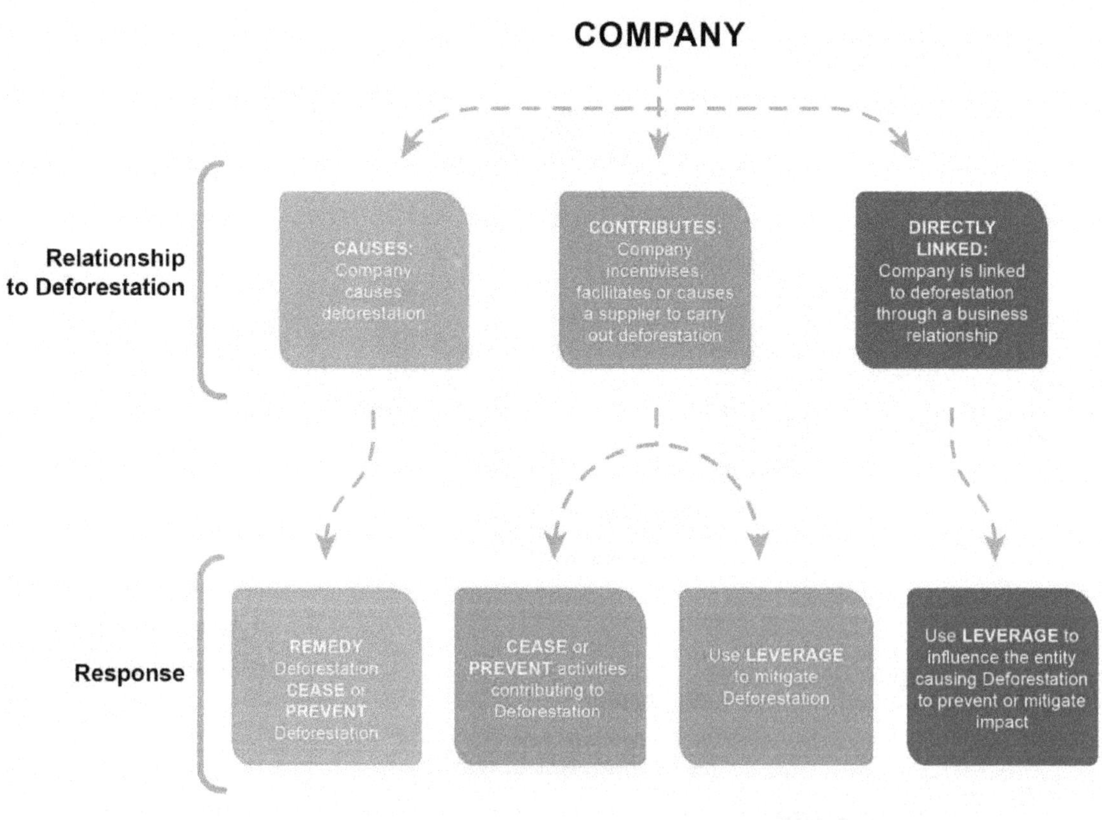

Source: Adapted from OECD (2018[18]), OECD Due Diligence Guidance for Responsible Business Conduct and OECD-FAO (2016[1]), OECD-FAO Guidance on Responsible Agricultural Supply Chains, Box 1.2.

An enterprise *causes* an adverse impact if the enterprise's actions by themselves result in the impact. For example, if an agricultural enterprise produces crops on land that it has cleared of forest, it is understood to cause that impact. Impacts can also result from inaction (omission).

An enterprise *contributes to* an adverse impact if its activities, in combination with the activities of other entities, result in the impact, or if the enterprise causes, facilitates or incentivises another entity to cause an adverse impact. Contribution must be substantial, meaning that this does not include minor or trivial contributions. For example, an agricultural company may be contributing if it acquires a land concession for development of a plantation, knowing that the land will need to be cleared of forests in order to grant the concession.

An enterprise *is directly linked to* an adverse impact when the impact is linked to its operations, products or services by a business relationship. An enterprise's business relationships include entities in the supply chain that are directly linked with its operations, products and services. Business relationships include relationships beyond contractual, first tier or immediate relationships. This could include for example a producer, processor or trader in the supply chain from which the enterprises receives its products or raw materials.

Step 1: Establish a policy on deforestation and strong management systems

Step 1 of the OECD-FAO Guidance is about establishing strong corporate management systems and policies, which in turn support all the subsequent steps of the OECD-FAO due diligence framework. This chapter outlines how Step 1 can help support companies' deforestation commitments.

Strategic questions for enterprises

- What level of ambition do we as a company have on deforestation? What is our definition of forests? Have we considered a deforestation cut-off date in our sourcing practices (see Glossary for definitions)?
- Does our policy meet or exceed legislation regarding forest protection in our home country, country of production and key export markets?
- Does our policy meet expectations from investors, legal advisors, local communities and civil society?
- Do senior executives in the company (including the Board) understand: (1) the commitments on deforestation the company has; (2) the ramifications of choosing a particular policy; (3) the systems required to implement such a policy (e.g. revising existing contracts and relationships, budget and personnel implications); and (4) the costs of not addressing deforestation for the company (direct or indirect impacts on production and revenues), and globally (in terms of climate change and biodiversity loss and the associated medium- and long-term insecurity of supply of agricultural commodities)?
- Has a lead focal point in the company been appointed to co-ordinate and manage the implementation of the due diligence approach to responsible sourcing (including on deforestation commitments), together with other company departments (e.g. legal, public/corporate affairs, procurement, marketing)? Is there adequate communication between them?
- Which suppliers and other stakeholders should we engage with in developing our commitments against deforestation? Do we have vulnerable producers, such as smallholders, in our supply chains that require specific support with compliance with the company's policy and regulatory requirements?
- Are company key performance indicators (KPIs) linked to achieving deforestation-related due diligence objectives part of our management systems?
- Which external due diligence systems or processes are we using to support our internal due diligence management (e.g. OECD-FAO Guidance, industry codes, commodity certification systems/schemes, audit protocols, etc.)?

Establish or update sustainability policies on deforestation and integrate into enterprise processes

The following key elements have been identified as important when developing a policy on deforestation:

- The policy applies across the entire company (including its subsidiaries) and its supply chains and ensures that all relevant departments work together to deliver a common commitment towards eliminating deforestation through responsible production and sourcing practices.
- It sets measurable targets for reducing deforestation and the risk of deforestation acceptable in the enterprise's operations, supply chains and business relationships. For example, the objective can be to achieve zero deforestation, or zero illegal deforestation, or a reduction in deforestation levels to be achieved by a specified date. The definition of the objective includes clear time-bound targets and cut-off dates and definitions of terms such as "forest", "deforestation" and "forest degradation" (see Glossary for definitions).

- Targets and definitions can often be derived from collective commitments the enterprise has entered into, international and national agreements and commitments, national legislation, industry association guidelines, the expectations of investors, or voluntary sustainability standards in certification systems (See Annex A for further resources).
- The policy is risk-based, meaning it addresses the most significant risks and impacts first, taking into consideration likelihood of an impact as well as the scale, scope and irremediable aspects of the impact.
- The policy is reviewed and adapted on a regular basis in light of new sourcing areas, shifting patterns of deforestation and increasing knowledge about deforestation risks in the supply chain and international standards and national legislation.

Embed policy on deforestation in oversight bodies and management systems and different company functions

Practices should be consistent throughout the operations of the enterprise, including in all the departments or units which may take decisions affecting commodities and products potentially associated with deforestation, including in particular the purchasing and procurement functions. The deforestation-related procedures should be consistent with, and integrated within, any other due diligence policies the enterprise may have.

Incorporate expectations and policies into engagement with suppliers and other business relationships

Since due diligence applies throughout an enterprise's supply chains and business relationships as well as to its own operations, regular communication with suppliers and other business partners is critical. For products and supply chains with associated high risk of deforestation, the enterprise should:

- Communicate key aspects of its policy on deforestation to suppliers and other relevant business relationships. Long-term relationships with business partners can increase leverage to encourage the adoption of such a policy and improve transparency.
- Include conditions and expectations on deforestation due diligence in supplier or business relationship contracts, supplier codes of conduct or other forms of written agreements, tailored to suppliers' capacities.
- Develop and implement pre-qualification processes on deforestation due diligence for suppliers and other business relationships, where feasible, adapting such processes to the specific risks and circumstances they face.
- Provide adequate resources, capacity-building and training to suppliers and other business relationships to help them understand and apply the policy and implement due diligence in relation to deforestation. This could include, for example, a standardised reporting framework for suppliers. Some suppliers, such as smallholder farmers, will need greater levels of support than others.
- Seek to understand and address barriers arising from the enterprise's way of doing business that may impede the ability of suppliers and other business relationships to implement the due diligence policy in relation to deforestation, such as the enterprise's purchasing practices and commercial incentives.

Enterprises may face practical and legal limitations to how they can influence or affect business relationships to prevent, cease, or mitigate adverse impacts on forests, or to remedy them. Enterprises can seek to overcome these challenges to influence business relationships through contractual arrangements, pre-qualification requirements, voting trusts, license or franchise agreements, and also through collaborative efforts to pool leverage in industry associations or cross-sectoral initiatives.

Implementation plans developed in co-ordination with business partners and involving, where appropriate, local and central governments, international organisations, local communities and civil society, can also improve compliance, in particular by offering capacity-building and training. Industry associations and multi-stakeholder initiatives may often be able to provide support for many of the steps described above.

Establish control systems along the supply chain

Establishing systems to enable the enterprise to monitor the implementation and impacts of its policy on deforestation is critical to the credibility and effectiveness of the policy and to good relationships with stakeholders, including investors and governments. This entails:

- Creating verification procedures to undertake regular independent and transparent reviews of compliance with the policy; this may include ongoing supplier engagement and monitoring, as well as internal and independent third-party audits (the latter is preferred where the risk of association with deforestation is higher), and covers both the enterprise and its suppliers.
- Establishing monitoring and control systems for the chains of custody of the commodities and products the enterprises identify as potentially associated with deforestation. This is described in more detail in Step 4 of the OECD-FAO Guidance (verifying due diligence).

Typically, these steps will take place at the same time, or soon after the enterprise has started to conduct supply chain mapping as per Step 2 of the OECD-FAO Guidance (identifying risks).

Establish an operational-level grievance mechanism, in consultation and collaboration with relevant stakeholders

Grievance mechanisms, which should include both early warning risk-awareness and complaints systems, can help alert enterprises to deviations from their policy on deforestation in their activities or those of their suppliers or other business relationships, help them to identify and mitigate risks, including by improved communication with stakeholders, and provide a mechanism to prevent and remediate conflicts. Grievance mechanisms can also incorporate a channel for feedback and suggestions. They can be established at the level of a project, an enterprise or an industry. Enterprises can both establish their own grievance mechanisms and participate in other grievance mechanisms. It is important that grievance mechanisms be accessible, especially, where relevant, to local stakeholders including women and other vulnerable and marginalised groups. Grievances should be handled within a reasonable timeframe and anonymity respected when requested.

Suggestions for SMEs

- Decide what level of policy commitment you are prepared to adopt given national laws and international commitments, and company commitments to customers.
- Choose the definitions of "forest" and "deforestation" you want to use and the cut-off date(s). (Sectoral initiatives or other SMEs' policies and commitments may provide useful models).
- Decide on how the policy commitment will be operationalised according to your financial and human resources.
- Make your commitments known; this can be through a written commitment or a stand-alone statement or as part of your business vision, value statement, or responsible sourcing policy.
- Engage in multi-stakeholder platforms on sustainable commodities that aim to minimise deforestation through collective action.
- Mention your limitations and risk prioritisation approach, including actions you will take if you discover that any business partner is sourcing from deforested areas.
- Reference national or regional commitments on deforestation and forest degradation in company policy.

Step 2: Identify, assess and prioritise deforestation risks in the supply chain

Step 2 of the OECD-FAO Guidance is about examining the supply chain and mapping the risks of deforestation within it, to enable enterprises to determine their priorities for action. Under the OECD-FAO Guidance, enterprises are expected to identify general areas where the risk of adverse impacts is most significant and to prioritise due diligence accordingly. High-risk suppliers or suppliers operating in high-risk areas will warrant more scrutiny.

Figure 5. Identify, assess and prioritise deforestation risks in the supply chain

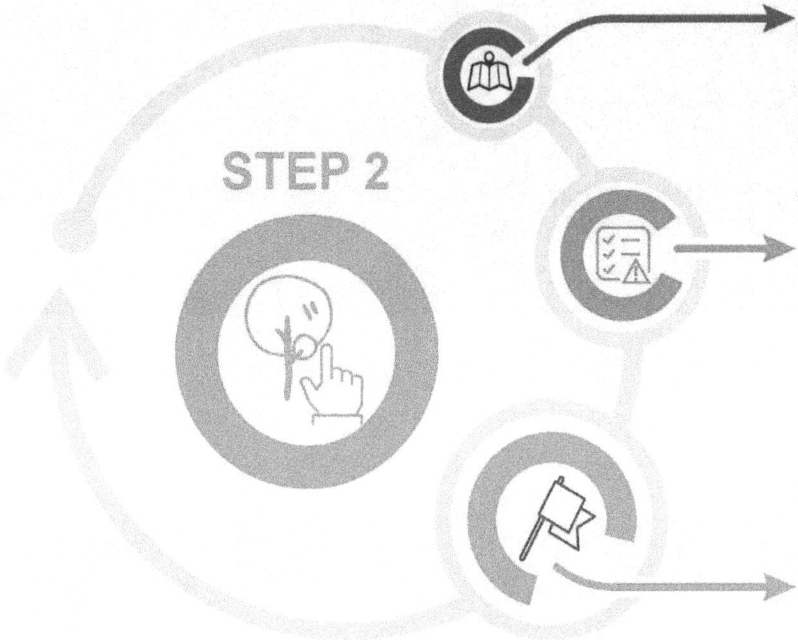

Map the supply chain

Identify the source of products and key actors. Identify "control points" to assess their due diligence efforts.

Assess the risks of deforestation

- Consider products, goods, services, suppliers and sourcing areas.
- Analyse extent/type of forest cover, deforestation trends and drivers of deforestation.
- Use traceability/chain of custody information to assess risks.

Look out for Red Flags

Examples:

- Areas with weak governance, law enforcement or conflict.
- Business partners/suppliers linked to deforestation.
- Suppliers sourcing from red-flag locations or red-flag suppliers.

Strategic questions for enterprises

Mapping the supply chain:

- Which departments within our company are responsible for supply chain mapping and prioritisation? Do they have the capacity and budget to meet company commitments on deforestation?
- What systems or processes do we currently have in place to map our operations and supply chains to identify deforestation risks (e.g. desk-based research, heat maps, supplier questionnaires, satellite data, field visits)?
    - How far upstream from our enterprise have we mapped the supply chain?
    - Do we have a plan to map the key control or "choke" points within those supply chains that are associated with high risks of deforestation? (See the Glossary)
    - Do we use a risk-based approach to prioritise which entities in the supply chain and which parts of the supply chain should be mapped in detail?
    - Are we ensuring that our identification efforts extend upstream to agricultural production?
    - Are there parts of the supply chain where mapping is impeded by a lack of transparency (e.g. purchases from the spot market)?
    - What can we do to increase transparency (e.g. engage with suppliers, stop buying from the spot market, etc.)?
- What level of traceability or chain of custody can we have in place for our products?
- Where does our information come from (e.g. internal systems/tracking, supplier feedback, external data; collaboration with industry groups, open-source deforestation satellite data)?
    - Do we have up-to-date maps on forest cover and deforestation frontiers in the areas from which we source our products and raw materials?
    - Which departments/individuals have responsibility for mapping deforestation risks and maintaining quality information? Do we rely on external public information for this or on a contract with a specific provider?
    - How reliable is this information, and how can we verify it?
    - How traceable are our commodities and products?
- What are our partners doing to identify deforestation risks? How can that information be strengthened, co-ordinated and streamlined in our approach?

Assess and prioritise the supply chain:

- What do we consider and define as the most salient or priority deforestation risks? Which are our highest risk suppliers or other business partners?
- What steps do we take to verify our supply chain data and ensure that it is current? Do we triangulate data, conduct supplier or site visits, conduct audits, use real-time data/tech, collaborate or exchange information with industry groups, etc.?
- Against which benchmarks and standards do we assess risks?
- How do we assess and prioritise the risks of deforestation? Do we use a system of "red flags" (see below)? Do we provide support to local farmers and enterprises, and what form does this take (i.e. training, resources, equipment)?

Map the supply chain by identifying the various actors involved, including immediate suppliers and business partners, and the sites of operation

Mapping and prioritizing should start with a high-level overview of company products, services and suppliers. This stage in the process involves establishing the sources of all the commodities and products covered by the enterprise's policy on deforestation, in order to understand at a high level the risks associated with their production and sourcing. The extent of information collected on suppliers and business partners depends on the severity of the deforestation risk and how closely they are linked to the identified risk.

Mapping the supply chain includes identifying:

- The source of the commodities or products derived from these commodities, including the country of production, source area and, where appropriate, the plot of land of production. This can help to identify the countries or areas most at risk of deforestation and enable the enterprise to focus on high-risk areas or suppliers in more detail. The legal and political context of the source area can be as important as trends in deforestation or agricultural production. Enterprises should carry out due diligence in locations which feature one or a combination of the following "red flags":
    - Areas defined or known as protected areas, collectively managed areas (under tenure rights of local communities or Indigenous Peoples), high conservation value areas, or high carbon stock areas (e.g. peat forests).
    - Areas with high levels of rural poverty and a reliance on agriculture as a main form of income.
    - Areas where local communities and Indigenous Peoples are present
    - Areas which are considered as at high risk of conflict
    - Weak protection of human rights, Indigenous Peoples' rights or poorly defined or contested land tenure rights (see Box 1)
    - Weak governance and implementation of the rule of law, and corruption
    - Weak levels of forest protection by national or local governments.

Box 1. Land tenure issues

Issues of land tenure (including the implied bundle of rights – from access to ownership) are central to the debates around halting deforestation. A significant portion of the world's remaining tropical forests are customarily owned by Indigenous Peoples and traditional communities and other customary rights-holders. Enterprises seeking to access land for commodity production must respect the rights of those who already own, occupy or otherwise use it. They may only acquire access to such land through a process that first recognises these rights. Sometimes this may also include national or local public authorities.

The rights of those without formal property rights to the lands should also be recognised; this includes those of tenants, sharecroppers, farm-workers, or those with informal rights to access and use land and natural resources. These informal rights can include women's tenure rights, which are commonly subsumed under those of the male head of household.

The tenure rights recognition process frequently poses challenges. It may not always be clear who has legal title to the land, customary rights may sometimes conflict with statutory rights, and statutory rights may sometimes not align with international human rights obligations. Many certification schemes and other tools (for example, the High Carbon Stock Approach), set out standards for respecting land tenure and processes for determining it, including, for example, participatory mapping carried out jointly by the enterprise and communities, although certification by itself does not always guarantee compliance with these standards.

Free, prior and informed consent (FPIC) can be an important element in this process. As set out in Annex B of the OECD-FAO Guidance, FPIC involves agreeing a consultation process with affected Indigenous Peoples; consulting and agreeing on what constitutes appropriate consent (taking into account representation of women and other marginalised groups); and engaging in the process of seeking consent before activities commence (if consent is given). This is an iterative and ongoing process rather than a one-off discussion; continuous dialogue will generate trust and a balanced agreement, or non-agreement, that will benefit the investment across all phases of the project, or provide a clear indication that it should not go ahead (FAO, 2014[19]; FAO, 2016[20])

More detail on responsible tenure governance is available in the *Voluntary Guidelines on the Responsible Governance of Tenure of Land, Fisheries and Forests in the Context of National Food Security* officially endorsed by the Committee on World Food Security in 2012.

In addition to red flag locations, companies can use a system of "red flags" for:

- Sectors or products – commodities known often to be linked to deforestation or forest degradation);
- Business partners – suppliers known to trade in commodities or source from forests; suppliers
    - Known to have a poor track record vis-a-vis deforestation
    - Known to have sourced commodities from red flag locations (see above)
    - Known to operate in red flag locations (see above)
    - Known not to have observed internationally agreed standards such as those contained in the OECD-FAO Guidance.

Companies can also prioritise certain products, geographies and suppliers to conduct further, more in-depth assessments. This approach helps companies to build transparency over the supply chain in those prioritised areas, products and suppliers.

Identifying the various actors involved in the supply chain, including suppliers and business partners and prioritizing using a risk-based approach. Such activities may be challenging if products are supplied through local traders or on spot markets. Mapping the supply chain will require dialogue with traders and suppliers, in particular those operating at the **control or choke points** of the supply chain. Enterprises can identify control points such as processing points where there are relatively few enterprises that handle a majority of inputs. Examples include commodity processors, commodity traders, wholesalers, exporters and/or commodity exchanges.

Repeating this process before making any new investments or pursuing business activities that result in changes in the supply chain.

Establishing a **system of controls and transparency** throughout the supply chain includes:

- Assessing the type and quality of supply-chain traceability or chain of custody offered by suppliers, and any complaints or grievances lodged against any of the actors in the supply chain, including suppliers and business partners.

- Approaches to traceability include tracing to origin; tracing to a supplier that has a robust traceability and due diligence system of its own (with the downstream company responsible for assessing the robustness of this system); tracing to a jurisdiction that can demonstrate a negligible risk of commodity-linked deforestation across the entire jurisdiction; and using a credible certification or chain of custody system.

The extent of information collected on suppliers and business partners depends on the severity of the deforestation risk and how closely linked to the identified risk they are. For areas at high risk of deforestation, a higher degree of traceability or chain of custody to the farm level will be needed; in some areas this will be challenging. The potential gap between the level of deforestation risk and the granularity of the information on the production area will need to be taken into account when defining the risk mitigation strategy.

Different traceability systems exist, including those used in many certification schemes (see Annex A for further information on Certification Schemes). Depending on the granularity of the information they monitor, they offer diverse levels of confidence regarding the link between the commodities and the place of production and hence the risk of deforestation:

- Under the *identity preserved* model, products from a single identifiable certified source are kept separate from uncertified products, and from certified products from other sources, throughout the supply chain. The plot of land of production is known.
- Under the *segregated* model, certified products from different certified sources are mixed together but kept separate from uncertified products.
- Under the *mass balance* model, certified products are mixed with uncertified products but the proportions are monitored administratively; users can advertise their product as partially certified (or mixed), usually with a specific percentage figure.
- Under the *book-and-claim* model, certified products are not kept apart, but suppliers of certified products sell credits to users; while the user may not actually be using any certified products, they do contribute to the costs of responsible production.

Box 2 lists the types and some potential sources of information needed by enterprises for these purposes.

Box 2. Types and potential sources of information to map the supply chain and assess deforestation risks

Types of information:

- Names and locations of farmers, local traders, processors and any other enterprises in the supply chain that a company further downstream wants to trace to
- Average production volumes of farms or jurisdictional area supplying the commodities, to detect possible leakages between production areas with different deforestation risks
- National production and trade data for the commodity in question; this may help in detecting possible leakages such as hidden imports from a third country in supply areas close to the borders
- Processing facility information (e.g. palm oil mill, soybean crusher sourcing areas)
- Where appropriate, geolocation data (geographic co-ordinates) of the plot of land on which the commodities are grown, by point co-ordinates or polygon mapping of the plot of production, farm boundaries or larger area, such as village or landscape or jurisdiction
- Farm mapping and registration databases
- Legal frameworks for the production of commodities and products purchased by the company and for forest conversion in the countries of production, levels of governance and law enforcement, legality compliance, respect for human rights and land rights, and corruption
- Certification scheme data, including, for example, volumes of products fully certified, and of products certified to more limited criteria
- Visual, isotopic or DNA analyses of samples (these can help distinguish between species, e.g. for timber, and, for some commodities, between different geographic origins)

Potential sources:

- Purchase orders and invoices, batch numbers of commodities and products
- Supplier questionnaires, including their sub-suppliers
- On-site visits to production, transformation and storage areas
- Company and industry association programmes, public summaries of audit reports and product claims or labels, including voluntary certification and legality verification schemes
- Information generated through jurisdictional or landscape approaches
- Private or public remote sensing providers
- Supply chain mapping and transparency tools, e.g. TRASE, SPOTT, FLEGT IMM, Open Timber Portal, commercial providers, sectoral initiatives, co-operation projects
- Traceability systems, e.g. commercial or national traceability systems, Independent Forest Monitoring, Timber Legality Assurance Systems
- Specific tools monitoring and assessing deforestation risk, e.g. Global Forest Watch
- Agriculture and trade statistics from national or international databases, e.g. FAOSTAT, UN Comtrade; land registries, and other sources of land data such as Land Matrix or Open Land Contracts.
- FAOLEX (a comprehensive legislative and policy database)

Note: All of the initiatives listed above approach deforestation according to different models or approaches; efforts should always be made to verify their reliability.

Assess risks of deforestation associated with the products, goods, services, suppliers and sourcing areas

Once the sources of the commodities and products covered by the enterprise's deforestation policy are identified, and the sourcing area is known, it becomes possible to assess the risk that their production has been associated with deforestation.

Likelihood and severity. The significance of an adverse impact is a function of its likelihood and its severity. The severity of impacts can be analysed according to their scale, scope and irremediable character:

- The *scale* of the adverse impact characterises the gravity of the impact on forests as a whole, or on particular types of forests (e.g. protected areas, high conservation value areas, high carbon stock areas) or the extent of changes in tree species composition.
- *Scope* concerns the reach of the impact, for example the extent of damage to the forest by total area or by impacts on specific areas or species.
- *Irremediable character* means any limits on the ability to restore the forest, or forest-dependent species, or the people living, working or depending on it, to a situation equivalent to their situation before the adverse impact. Special attention should be paid to the substantial challenges of restoring the social and environmental values and functions of a forest.

The process of prioritisation is ongoing, and in some instances new or emerging adverse impacts may arise and be prioritised before moving on to less significant impacts.

The risk assessment should combine information on:

- Extent and type of forest cover in the sourcing area
- Trends of deforestation in this area (in general, not just for specific products)
- Information on direct drivers of deforestation
- Information on indirect drivers of deforestation
- Levels of traceability
- Complexity of the supply chain

The higher the extent and risk of deforestation, the greater the level of detail that will be needed. Where the risk is very low, an assessment at the country or regional level may be adequate; where it is higher, the assessment will need to focus on smaller areas, and may require detailed geolocation information to the farm level. Addressing any information gaps for high-risk source areas should be a high priority.

Forest cover. This should include assessments of the proximity of suppliers to remaining forest land within the supply area (including within the farms themselves) and adjacent to it, which should help the enterprise to assess the risk of future deforestation. For example, a region with low rates of deforestation but with a significant amount of standing forest is a higher risk compared to a region with previously high rates of deforestation but no forest left.

Deforestation trends. An increasing range of sources of information on deforestation rates and incidences are now available (see Box 3 and the Glossary). Deforestation fronts move over time and their dynamics are not linear. The risk of deforestation in supply areas (which may themselves often change) should therefore be updated on a regular basis, and the use of deforestation alert services should be considered.

Direct drivers. A direct driver of deforestation is the direct cause of the forest loss and associated land use change. Estimating the likelihood of the conversion of forests to cropland or grassland being caused by the extension of production of the commodity used by the enterprise is a key element of the risk assessment.

Underlying/Indirect drivers. Indirect drivers, sometimes called underlying drivers, include the policy, legal, economic, social or contextual causes that induced the land use change. For instance, if the evidence shows that an increased demand and/or increased prices for a specific commodity have driven deforestation, and commercial forecasts indicate that this trend will remain, then the risk of deforestation will remain high. For another example, where standards of forest and land use governance and law enforcement are weak, the risk of deforestation will be higher than where they are stronger.

The complexity of the supply chain, including the number of intermediate steps within it, and the risk of mixing of products from unknown or potentially high-risk sources. This includes identifying the various actors involved in the supply chain, including suppliers and business partners. This is important: the greater the number of links in the chain, the higher is the risk, since every link potentially increases the chance of products associated with deforestation entering supplies. The type of links – e.g. intermediary traders sourcing directly from farms and selling the commodities on to the next link in the supply chain – are also important, particularly where the commodity is obtained from a large number of sources such as smallholder farmers, who may need support in complying with the enterprise's policy.

Where it is not feasible to address all identified impacts, an enterprise should prioritise action based on the severity and likelihood of the adverse impact. Once the most significant impacts are identified and dealt with, the enterprise should move on to address less significant impacts.

Box 3. Potential sources of information on deforestation and deforestation drivers

- Remote sensing through satellite or radar data, e.g. Global Forest Watch, Terra-i, Earth Resources Observation and Science (EROS) Center; national systems (e.g. PRODES, Brazil; Mapbiomas; IDEAM, Colombia; Geobosques, Peru)
- Assessments of the status of governance and law enforcement in the source country, e.g. World Bank Worldwide Governance Indicators, Transparency International Corruption Perceptions Index or Freedom House Index
- Deforestation alerts, e.g. Global Forest Watch GLAD alerts, RADD Forest Disturbance Alert
- FAO Forest Resources Assessment series
- Local communities, Indigenous Peoples and civil society organisations; Independent or community forest monitors (empowering community members to act as forest monitors can be an effective way to collect data and raise the alarm on deforestation)
- Country or landscape risk assessments, e.g. those conducted by LandScale
- Information collected through early warning and grievance mechanisms
- Studies of deforestation drivers, Measuring Reporting and Verification (MRV) reports, e.g. in national REDD+ strategies
- Tools provided by civil society, e.g. the Cocoa Accountability Map by Mighty Earth
- For further resources please see Annex A.

Risk assessments: what types are there and who does what?

Several types and levels of risk assessments are possible.

- **Context risk assessments:** At country or regional level, by assessing the regulatory framework, political context, civil liberties and socio-economic environments.
- **Site-level risk assessments** aim to understand the factual circumstances of the operations of business partners in order to assess the scope, severity and likelihood of risks at the site level.

Assessments can include checking volumes of commodities produced in particular areas against allowable volumes, undertaking stakeholder consultations, monitoring by third parties such as civil society organisations, and organising visits to the farms and/or processing facilities.

- **Upstream enterprises** (such as farms and plantations) may establish on-the-ground assessment teams for generating and sharing verifiable, reliable and up-to-date information on the extent of deforestation. These enterprises also need to ensure that they respect legitimate land tenure right holders (see Box 1). They should provide the results of their risk assessments to downstream enterprises.
- **Downstream enterprises** should not only identify risks in their own operations but also, to the best of their efforts, assess the risks faced by their suppliers and sub-suppliers. They can evaluate the latter by assessing the due diligence carried out by their suppliers or by directly assessing the operations of their suppliers, for instance by conducting visits to farms and local communities. Tools such as deforestation alerts can help to spot-check suppliers' operations for potential association with deforestation. Information should be sought both on the suppliers' systems and the volumes of products they are supplying. Participating in industry-wide schemes that assess the compliance of business partners with deforestation policies and provide relevant information can support these assessments.
- **Financial enterprises** should carry out due diligence with regard to their clients and investments. The nature and extent of the due diligence will depend on the size and nature of the enterprise's investment portfolio and its relationship to specific clients and investments (e.g. the ownership share in the company, tenure of investment, access to relevant information and the likelihood that meaningful influence may be exercised). Where financial enterprises have large numbers of clients and investee companies, they are encouraged to prioritise efforts based on risk assessments. Financial enterprises should seek to prioritise the most severe deforestation-related impacts for due diligence while continuing to monitor risks, evaluate prioritisation decisions and build on their actions to the extent possible and necessary over time, to cover a broader range of clients and investee companies and actions.

Suggestions for SMEs

All SMEs:

- Identify your commodity focus and prioritise your mapping efforts accordingly.
- Create a list of your direct and indirect (outsourced) suppliers and identify which ones may require greater scrutiny/due diligence actions in terms of deforestation (by geography/location, type of commodity, parts of supply chain, company size).
- Information on direct and indirect suppliers can be collected in a variety of different ways to minimise costs, including desk-based research using existing publicly disclosed information online, working with third-party initiatives or certification schemes, working collectively as part of industry associations. Some industry collaborations allow SMEs to share risk assessment, traceability and sometimes monitoring information.
- Ask your direct suppliers to send you information on their due diligence practices, sourcing practices and deforestation policies; assess those approaches to better understand which suppliers may not have effective measures to consider deforestation risks.
- Consider having regular calls, or check-ins with upstream suppliers operating at control points of the supply chain to better understand how they are identifying, preventing and mitigating deforestation impacts in the commodities that you have prioritised.

In addition, upstream SMEs can:

- Know where your product comes from, and how it is grown and sourced; it may be more feasible to focus on particular source landscapes rather than wider areas.
- Hold meetings with cooperatives, farmers or other producers, and Indigenous Peoples and local communities, who are at the front lines of production and deforestation risks.
- Build your leverage: collaborate with other SMEs that source from the same producers to identify and prioritise deforestation risks in the sector.
- Seek advice and information from business associations, certification schemes (private or national), international organisations (e.g. OECD, FAO, UNEP), government entities, NGOs, trade unions and relevant multi-stakeholder initiatives.

Step 3: Design and implement a strategy to respond to deforestation

Step 3 of the OECD-FAO Guidance is about responding to the findings of risks of deforestation through reporting to designated senior management and designing and adopting a risk management plan. The plan should cover appropriate risk mitigation and prevention measures. Enterprises should ensure that risks are addressed, and that they are taking steps to tackle adverse impacts that have occurred.

Figure 6. Design and implement a strategy to respond to deforestation

Strategic questions for enterprises

Designing the strategy

- Do we have a strategy with clear actions to respond to the identified deforestation risks? How often do we need to update it?
- What activities do we have the capacity to undertake in response to deforestation risks and impacts, and any forthcoming legislation?
- How have we engaged with external stakeholders in developing our strategy?
- How do we ensure that our strategy is up to date and working – e.g. through an annual review process, or collaboration with industry players?
- To what extent can we work directly with producers? What assistance and support do they need (with special attention being paid to independent and contracted smallholders)?
- Do we understand when we need to offer remedy (e.g. "cause" cases)? Have we considered the types of remedy that we could offer?
- What steps can we take to innovate in our risk mitigation plans? Issues include the role of technology, cross-sector collaboration, engagement with governments at different stages of the supply chain, engagement with Indigenous Peoples and local communities.

Implementing the strategy

- Who within our company is responsible and accountable for the implementation of this strategy? Have we identified people in each department who are responsible for doing their part to reduce the identified risk? How is the Board kept apprised of our actions?
- Do we have an in-country or regional presence, or will we have to bring in a third party to implement activities on our behalf? How often do they report back on progress?
- What steps can we take to increase overall leverage in the supply chain to change the business behaviour of suppliers and address root causes of deforestation (e.g. are we engaging with governments and organisations in producing countries, including OECD National Contact Points for RBC and FAO country focal points)?
- To what extent do we need external partners to create impact on the ground?
- How is the progress and impact of our risk mitigation strategy measured and rewarded?

Define and adopt a risk management plan

Having assessed the risk of association of the enterprise's operations and supply chains with deforestation, the next stage is to cease causing harm or mitigate the risk and prevent future risks. All the related measures and processes should be defined in a risk management plan; separate plans may be necessary for different commodities or different sourcing areas.

Box 4 includes potential risk prevention measures which can help manage the risk of deforestation in the enterprise's operations and supply chains, and companies should refer to the OECD-FAO Guidance for more detail.

Box 4. Risk prevention measures

Risk prevention measures available to enterprises will depend on their position in the supply chain and their capacity; some of the measures below are applicable mainly to producers and some to enterprises sourcing directly from producers.

Measures to improve transparency and the level of information available include:

- Requiring more than one source of information on products (see Box 2 and Box 3)
- Undertaking independent surveys or audits of source areas and/or business partners
- Commissioning an independent audit of the enterprise's due diligence system
- Conducting audits of suppliers' due diligence systems, focusing on their systems to identify and address deforestation risks
- Reinforcing traceability or chain of custody systems and engaging with control points in key commodity chains
- Empowering local community members to act as forest monitors
- Using certification schemes (with careful evaluation of actual consideration of forest protection in the selected scheme)
- Potentially sharing information on risks and risk mitigation strategies with other companies through industry associations or public-private platforms; this is likely to be of particular value to SMEs
- Communicating regularly with OECD National Contact Points for RBC.

Measures to engage with suppliers include improving awareness, and offering assistance and incentives, especially for smallholder farmers, particularly those affected by any deforestation cut-off date the company is implementing or that is required by regulation.

- Providing financial support, longer-term contracts
- Responsible purchasing practices
- Better payment terms
- Access to forestry experts or due diligence experts
- Capacity-building and training. Sometimes such support may be better delivered by local NGOs or other organisations.

The risk management plan should specify:

- Timelines for developing each of the measures and processes to be adopted.
- Resources to be mobilised, including budgetary (for travels, data procurement, traceability system, etc.) and human (forestry experts and legal experts, for example).
- Roles and responsibilities within the enterprise for implementing the management measures (e.g. who on the Board could be a resource for responding to deforestation issues, participation of teams on procurement, regional heads of areas that include red flag locations, etc.?).
- Procedures for consulting with affected stakeholders, including business partners, governments and affected communities and civil society in the countries of origin, to clarify concerns and agree on the strategy for mitigating risks and opportunities to feed into the deforestation policies and strategy of the company.

- Monitoring systems for assessing the implementation of the plan and its impacts (including, for example, access to publicly available data/satellite monitoring of forests, indicators/ data points to collect from suppliers), and reporting processes to designated senior management.
- Procedures to follow in cases of non-compliance by suppliers and follow-up plans such as awareness-raising, training on detection and reporting on deforestation.
- Procedures to support producers, notably smallholders, with attention to gender and social inclusion.

Respond to adverse impacts – implement the risk management plan, monitor and track performance

How an enterprise responds to adverse impacts will depend on the extent to which it causes, contributes to or is directly linked to them. In the specific case of deforestation, it means the following:

If the enterprise has caused deforestation, it should cease the activities that cause deforestation, prevent further potential adverse impacts and provide remedy for actual adverse impacts it caused. This may entail suspending operations temporarily while undertaking measurable efforts to prevent any future adverse impacts, or suspending operations permanently if these impacts cannot be mitigated.

Where assessment and mapping exercises find that the enterprise has contributed to deforestation, it should cease and provide remedy with respect to its contribution and use its leverage over its business partners to mitigate any remaining adverse impacts. This may entail suspending operations temporarily. The enterprise should also take preventive measures to ensure that these adverse impacts do not recur.

If the enterprise has not contributed to deforestation, but an observed impact has nevertheless been directly linked to its operations, products or services through a business relationship, it should use its leverage to mitigate or prevent the adverse impact, for instance requesting changes in the investment plan to ensure that forests are preserved and sustainable production practices are encouraged. This may lead to disengaging from a business partner after failed attempts at mitigating risks or when risk mitigation is deemed to be not feasible or unacceptable.

Where it is possible, continue the relationship and demonstrate a realistic prospect of, or actual improvement over time, such an approach will often be preferable to disengagement. The enterprise should also take into account potential social, environmental and economic adverse impacts related to the decision to disengage. When deciding to disengage, enterprises should do so responsibly including by seeking meaningful consultation with relevant stakeholders in a timely manner and where possible, by taking reasonable and appropriate measures to prevent or mitigate adverse impacts related to their disengagement.

Factors that are relevant to determining the appropriate response include: the severity of the adverse impact, the enterprise's ability to influence and/or build leverage over the business partner or other relevant actors (e.g. government), and how critical the business partner is to the enterprise (if it is critical, the enterprise should increase its efforts to change the partner's behaviour; where is it less crucial, disengagement may be a better option). A wide range of measures are available to enterprises to mitigate the adverse impacts of deforestation, depending on the enterprise's position in the supply chain. Where feasible they should encompass measures that achieve positive impacts on forests and the workers and communities who depend on them – what are sometimes termed "forest-positive" actions.

Responding to deforestation impacts and promoting forest-positive outcomes

Actions to protect and restore forests include:

- Identifying areas of future risk to forests in or near the enterprise's supply chains and engaging suppliers to take preventive action. This could include, for example, engaging with farmers to understand why deforestation may occur and what measures could be adopted to ensure it does not.
- Investing in programmes that promote forest conservation and sustainable agricultural production practices, such as agroforestry and intercropping.
- Supporting forest ecosystem restoration in areas of degraded forest, and the restoration and sustainable use of fallow or degraded land.
- Choosing to buy from suppliers who are implementing forest-positive practices themselves, including conserving and restoring forests while promoting sustainable livelihoods.
- Rewarding such suppliers by purchasing their goods at a premium, buying larger quantities or agreeing longer-term contracts.

Working with farmers, farmer cooperatives and local communities, who are central to managing forest conservation and restoration, could include:

- Making and communicating explicit commitments to respecting the rights of Indigenous Peoples and local communities (See Annex B of the OECD-FAO Guidance: Engagement with Indigenous Peoples. (OECD-FAO, 2016[1]))
- Gathering information on land tenure (both statutory and customary rights) within the enterprise's operations and supply chains and those of its suppliers, and adopting measures to ensure they are not adversely affected by the enterprise's operations.
- Supporting innovation and capacity-building to improve agricultural productivity and diversified production systems including agroforestry and farm management systems in order to help reduce poverty and meet community food security needs without expansion into forests.
- Providing support to farmers, particularly smallholders, in adopting agricultural innovation and sustainable, forest-positive techniques and technologies, so that incomes are strengthened, farms are more productive and resilient and forests are kept standing.
- Paying farmers and farm organisations (such as co-operatives and women's producer organisations) fair prices for their products, with the aim of contributing to achieving living incomes – potentially linked to performance in reducing deforestation and forest degradation, adopting sustainable production techniques, and engaging in forest ecosystem restoration.
- Supporting smallholder livelihood initiatives that deliver forest conservation and farmer resilience and inclusion, including through long-term contracts, responsible purchasing practices, strengthening organisational structures such as cooperatives, implementing traceability systems and financial support.
- Encouraging and supporting local initiatives, involving farmers, local communities, Indigenous Peoples, women and other marginalised groups, local industry and government, to develop and implement local solutions.
- Collaborating with local government to jointly foster enabling framework conditions for deforestation-free production, such as clarifying and recognising land rights and providing targeted support by agricultural extension officers.
- Participating in or developing systems of payments for ecosystem services.

Supporting landscape and jurisdictional initiatives to help address the root causes of deforestation in particular regions could include:

- Contributing to the development of forest-positive strategies across an entire landscape or jurisdiction – measures include improving land use planning, identifying no-go areas, strengthening forest monitoring by public authorities and/or local communities, helping companies avoid deforestation and manage conservation areas.
- Helping to promote collaboration amongst the private sector within the landscape or jurisdiction, and with governments, communities, Indigenous Peoples and sources of financial support and investment.
- Supporting local forest monitors and environmental defenders.
- Supporting initiatives and stakeholders engaged in improving law enforcement.
- Supporting and lobbying for improvements in the wider enabling environment, including, for example, greater supply chain transparency, traceability and monitoring systems; improvements in governance and law enforcement, particularly in human rights and land rights; and the wider provision of agricultural support, infrastructure and public services, with appropriate support from donors and national and local public entities.
- Participating in the development of sustainable finance mechanisms for conservation and restoration initiatives that include social and environmental co-benefits, including improved biodiversity and more resilient livelihoods and respect for human rights.

Promoting and supporting international initiatives to reduce deforestation and scale up forest-positive action could include:

- Encouraging and participating in the development of commodity roundtables, certification schemes and other multi-stakeholder initiatives.
- Participating in appropriate industry initiatives, business associations and coalitions.
- Supporting the development of reliable and accessible sources of data on deforestation rates and drivers, and examples of best forest-positive practice.
- Contributing to the dissemination of information and knowledge on international initiatives, regulations and schemes, notably on processes linked to the REDD+ framework.

Suggestions for SMEs

All SMEs:

- Designate someone in your company to lead and decide who should be involved in designing and implementing your strategy; ensure they have the sufficient resources, knowledge and support.
- Tap into industry initiatives and association networks to learn how peers and other companies are addressing problems and if they have similar approaches that can guide your efforts.
- Include deforestation targets and objectives as part of performance reviews and incentives for staff, to drive change.
- Ensure that your identified risks feature in sales terms, procurement and contracting practices and in clauses in your agreements.
- Identify the resources needed to implement the activities under your risk management plan.
- Share your action plan with all your suppliers and ask your suppliers also to share it with partners in the supply chain with whom you may not have direct contact.
- Explain to suppliers that may be identified in your prioritisation efforts that you will need to enhance co-operation in reducing deforestation risk.

In addition, upstream SMEs can:

- Consider including in your strategy actions to develop co-operation with producers, smallholder farmers, Indigenous Peoples, local communities or other stakeholders in the supply chain, and communicate that strategy downstream.
- Include requests on due diligence that customers ask for, to help shape your strategy.

Step 4: Verify due diligence of deforestation

Step 4 of the OECD-FAO Guidance is about establishing systems to track and monitor due diligence actions to make sure they are effective.

Strategic questions for enterprises

- Do we conduct due diligence assessments at key points in the supply chain (i.e. at control or choke points)?
- Are our due diligence assessments internally led or carried out by external third-party assessors, or both? Have we used external audits for any gaps to ensure that the assessment is comprehensive and considers different ways that deforestation occurs (e.g. through outsourcing to different suppliers, etc.)? If so, have we checked the independence and quality of those audits and the information flowing from them, and layered on our own risk-based monitoring and verification activities?
- What role can technology play in assessments of our due diligence actions on deforestation?
- Are there opportunities to partner with others in sharing data and reducing costs?
- How have we responded to third parties' complaints on deforestation risks?
- If we use third party commodity or product certification schemes, do we know if these schemes are aligned to the OECD-FAO Guidance and the risk-based due diligence framework? If not, what steps can we take to make sure they are more aligned?
- How do we monitor suppliers with whom we do not have a contract, in order to effect change?

Track the implementation and effectiveness of due diligence activities

Enterprises should take steps to verify that their due diligence practices are effective, i.e. that risks have been adequately identified and prevented and adverse impacts have been mitigated. This involves both *monitoring* of impacts to assess and document the extent to which actions, progress, performance and compliance are being carried out or achieved; and *verification* of compliance, performance, and/or actions relative to a stated commitment, standard or target.

This process should be proportionate to the risk; take into account the capacities of various enterprises, as such processes can be costly; and where necessary, generate recommendations to improve due diligence practices.

Monitoring of the effectiveness of the enterprise's due diligence process can draw on the types of information listed in Chapter 5 on types and potential sources of information on commodities and products; and on sources of information on deforestation. This monitoring should consider the following:

- Levels of deforestation, and levels of the risk of deforestation, in the areas from which the enterprise is sourcing commodities and products change over time and need to be continually monitored. The elements listed in Box 2 (on types and potential sources of information on commodities and products) will help to deliver information on the products and commodities in the enterprise's operations and supply chains.
- The sources listed in Box 3 can help to identify deforestation in the supply area during the monitored period: any change in tree cover in this area constitutes an alert for which the level of the enterprise's responsibility must be assessed.

Verification of the effects of the enterprise's due diligence procedure include reviews of documents and internal control mechanisms, verification via satellite data, third-party audits,[5] on-site investigations, and consultations with local communities, civil society and government authorities. The frequency and intensity of verification efforts should themselves be risk-based, in line with Step 2 of the OECD-FAO Guidance (identifying risks).

The results of monitoring and verification efforts should be fed back into the design and functioning of the due diligence system, as due diligence is a dynamic process. Where the risk has been mitigated or prevented, the enterprise should conduct ongoing due diligence to ensure that the risk does not recur, or that new risks do not appear.

The enterprise should also monitor its own internal control mechanisms and ensure they are robust and working as intended. Consultation and engagement with external stakeholders such as Indigenous Peoples, local communities, civil society and international organisations can help to identify problems and is crucial to the impartial and efficient verification of due diligence processes.

Suggestions for SMEs

All SMEs:

- Identify local NGOs and communities or international organisations with knowledge of the agricultural sourcing communities in your focus commodity sectors; speak to them regularly to triangulate information you receive from suppliers.
- Understand from your customers or existing regulations the type and frequency of data needed. Seek ways in which data can be pooled across customers, or how technology can be used to increase efficiency and reduce costs.
- Consult existing platforms that can help you to identify deforestation alerts in your supply areas.
- Consider working with partners and suppliers to introduce joint complaints or whistleblowing systems. The OECD National Contact Points for RBC can also be a resource in this regard.
- Consider using tools and indicators from industry initiatives, certification schemes, or deforestation platforms that you may be part of, to support your verification of due diligence.
- Work together with peer companies and industry groups to increase your leverage when deforestation risks persist within your supply chains.
- Team up with other suppliers, business associations and NGOs, if your leverage over a business partner is insufficient to encourage change.

In addition, upstream SMEs can:

- Ensure that your customers know how you verify and collect information, including the type of data collected, frequency of collection and who you work with in obtaining that data.
- Be transparent in communicating what information you do not have, and why.
- Discuss with upstream buyers how they may support your data collection activities and use their leverage and capacity, which may be greater than your own.
- Identify and support existing forest monitoring systems for your areas of supply whether based on community monitoring or remote sensing surveys.

Step 5: Report on due diligence to address deforestation

Step 5 of the OECD-FAO Guidance is about reporting publicly on company efforts to implement due diligence.

Strategic questions for enterprises

- Do we report on deforestation risks identified in our supply chain and specific mitigation we have undertaken?
- Do we provide an annual update on our deforestation commitments and how we are progressing (or not) against them?
- Should our reporting be carried out through one document or through several discrete issue reports linked to our company deforestation commitments, or the commodities we handle, or through a chapter in our company report on sustainability?
- Have we incorporated the reporting recommendations according to the OECD-FAO Guidance?
- Do we share these reports with external stakeholders, and ask for candid feedback on what is good and what can be improved?
- How do our reports on due diligence contribute to improving our overall learning and improvement of due diligence to address deforestation?
- Do we publicly disclose our efforts on the different due diligence steps, including co-operation with suppliers to mitigate deforestation risks from taking place?

Public Reporting

It is important that enterprises with exposure to actual or potential deforestation risks publicly and regularly report on their forest-related due diligence policies and practices (where appropriate as part of a wider framework, such as deforestation- and conversion-free objectives), with due regard taken to business confidentiality and other competitive concerns. This may include both qualitative information on system design and quantitative reporting on performance. This can provide affected stakeholders, business partners and investors with clear, accurate and timely information on actual and potential adverse impacts identified through ongoing impact assessments, and on the steps and measures taken to mitigate or prevent them.

Information that could feature in such reports includes:

- The enterprise's commitments with regard to tackling deforestation and forest degradation, including not only the objectives (no deforestation or reduction of risk by a defined percentage, etc.) but also the enterprise's definition of forests, deforestation and forest degradation, cut-off dates, scope in terms of commodities and geographies, and so on.
- The percentage of the enterprise's production volume (both from land managed by the enterprise and sourced) that is determined to be deforestation-free or the percentage for which this not known.
- Summaries of the data and information collected, outlining the enterprise's exposure to risks, progress made against each target and commitment (preferably in a time series, showing progress year by year) and any adverse impacts it may have caused or contributed to.
- The enterprise's management systems, including its due diligence policy, specifying the management structure responsible for the company's due diligence and who in the company is directly responsible.
- The risk analysis and mitigation systems put in place by the enterprise to address deforestation, including how they function and the control systems in place, including certification, traceability or chain of custody.

- How the information collected has been used to strengthen responsible sourcing and management, mitigate against risks, provide remediation and meet the enterprise's commitments.
- Co-operation with stakeholders and methods for disclosing information to all clients and suppliers, upstream and downstream, including in the context of identifying or managing the drivers of deforestation
- Information on compliance with any national legislative requirements and international standards on due diligence and deforestation.

Reporting on the enterprise's due diligence systems and performance can take place in various contexts and formats, including the company's annual reports, sustainability reports or specific reports on the enterprise's impacts on forests. Reports can be made publicly available through the enterprise's website, social media and meetings with stakeholders, including upstream and downstream partners. Communication needs to be appropriate to the impacts and audience in terms of its form (including translation into appropriate languages), frequency, accessibility, and the adequacy of information provided. Information collected can also be communicated to reporting frameworks, such as CDP Forests' disclosure system, the Global Reporting Initiative (GRI) reporting standards, the supply-change.org website or national or international trade associations and groupings.

Reports should adopt clear and constant metrics, to facilitate monitoring and analysis at supply chain or country level, for instance. Enterprises should report on the outcomes of processes in all the due diligence steps, in line with the OECD-FAO Guidance; doing so could also contribute to alignment with reporting standards such as those of the GRI. For instance, with respect to step 1, enterprises could describe their policy commitments for RBC, provide links to these commitments (if publicly available, or, if not, explain the reason for this), report the level at which each of the policy commitments was approved within the organisation, including whether this is the most senior level, report the extent to which the policy commitments apply to the enterprise's activities and to its business relationships, and describe how the policy commitments are communicated to workers, business partners, and other relevant parties. Moreover, enterprises should describe how they embed each of their policy commitments for RBC throughout their activities and business relationships.

Suggestions for SMEs

All SMEs:

- Decide how and when you want to communicate with your customers and business partners in the most resource efficient way; this can take place via email and supported by social media.
- Include relevant information on deforestation risks you identified and mitigation efforts in your annual reports, if you produce them.
- If your business participates in sub-national, national or international certification or forest protection initiatives, communicate your efforts to mitigate deforestation risks according to the OECD-FAO Guidance and this Handbook.

In addition, upstream SMEs can:

Consider making use of shorter regular updates posted on your premises, website or via social media.

Remediation for adverse impacts

This chapter of the Handbook addresses what actions an enterprise can take when it has failed to prevent or mitigate deforestation, including remediation.

While the prevention of deforestation should take priority, there may be cases where an enterprise, though its exercise of due diligence or other means, has identified actual deforestation but has failed to prevent or mitigate it entirely. In such a case the enterprise should identify why, and take remedial action in relation to any adverse impacts which have resulted.

The enterprise should identify why its due diligence procedures failed to prevent or mitigate the adverse impacts and take corrective action to ensure that the problem does not recur; engagement with local stakeholders, including local communities and Indigenous Peoples, civil society and government, will be essential in establishing suitable mechanisms.

When an enterprise identifies that it has caused or contributed to actual adverse impacts, a number of measures can be taken:

- Where possible, the enterprise should seek to restore the *affected person or persons* to the situation they would be in had the adverse impact not occurred. This may include, where possible, the restitution of land to dispossessed Indigenous Peoples or local communities.
- Where possible, the enterprise should seek to restore *the affected environment* to the state it would be in had the adverse impact not occurred, e.g. by restoring degraded forests or deforested land, and ensuring long-term support for the restored area.
- Where this is not possible (in many cases of deforestation it may not be), the enterprise can: (1) provide appropriate levels of compensation in a form mutually agreed by affected communities (this may not always be monetary; a community could identify support for education or health services, for example, as more appropriate); and/or (2) provide appropriate compensation for environmental impacts, in particular greenhouse gas emissions and biodiversity loss.
- Where appropriate, the enterprise can provide for or cooperate with legitimate remediation mechanisms through which impacted stakeholders and rights-holders can raise complaints and seek to have them addressed with the enterprise (see also section on grievance mechanisms in Step 1 of the OECD-FAO Guidance).

Glossary

Definitions marked with an asterisk (*) are the standard definitions established by the FAO (2020[21]); others are not internationally agreed. Although they also feature in many international and national frameworks and legislation, it is important to note that definitions of some of these terms, such as "forest", are often different in national legislation and in voluntary standards. Companies can adopt different definitions but should ensure they are clearly stated in their corporate strategy on deforestation.

Afforestation: Establishment of forest through planting and/or deliberate seeding on land that, until then, was under a different land use, implies a transformation of land use form non-forest to forest.

Control points or choke points: Enterprises that have greater visibility and/or leverage over their own suppliers and over business relationships further up the supply chain than enterprises closer towards consumers or end-users. They can have the following characteristics:

- Point of transformation. They are located at key points of transformation in the supply chain where traceability or chain of custody information may be aggregated or lost.
- Low number. There are relatively few enterprises at this specific point in the supply chain that process or handle a majority of inputs that they pass further down or up into the chain.
- High Leverage. The greatest point of leverage over suppliers and actors further upstream in the supply chain.
- Audits occur here. Points where schemes and audit programmes already exist to leverage these systems and avoid duplication.

Conversion: Change of a forest or other natural ecosystem to another land use or profound change in a natural ecosystem's species composition, structure, or function.

Cut-off date: The date in legislation or standard after which deforestation on the plots or properties of origin is not permitted if the commodities or products are to be considered compliant with the legislation or standard or policy.

Deforestation*: The conversion of forest to other land use independently, whether human-induced or not.

Deforestation-free: There is no standard definition for this term, but it is generally taken to mean commodities or products or supply chains that do not cause or contribute to deforestation or forest degradation in their country of origin.

Forest*: Land spanning more than 0.5 hectares with trees higher than 5 metres and a canopy cover of more than 10%, or trees able to reach these thresholds in situ. It does not include land that is predominantly under agricultural or urban land use.

Forest degradation: There is no FAO or other standard definition for this term; the FAO encourages countries to define it themselves. The definition included in the Accountability Framework, which applies to other natural ecosystems as well as forests, is: "Changes within a natural ecosystem that significantly and negatively affect its species composition, structure, and/or function and reduce the ecosystem's capacity to supply products, support biodiversity, and/or deliver ecosystem services." (Accountability Framework, 2020[4])

Forest-positive: There is no single definition for this term, but it is generally taken to mean moving beyond simply managing deforestation risks in an enterprise's supply chain to achieving positive impacts on forests and the workers and communities who depend on them.

High carbon stock approach: methodology for distinguishing forest areas that should be protected – those that are important to local communities or have high carbon or biodiversity values – from degraded lands that may be developed, through an integrated land use planning approach.

High conservation value: biological, ecological, social, or cultural value of outstanding significance or critical importance.

Indigenous Peoples*: People regarded as indigenous on account of their descent from the population which inhabited the country, or a geographical region to which the country belongs, at a time of conquest or colonisation or the establishment of present state boundaries and who, irrespective of their legal status, retain some or all of their own social, economic, cultural and political institutions.

Landscape and Jurisdictional Approaches: IUCN defines a Landscape approach as one where the interests of the different stakeholders in a landscape are assessed in an integral manner and aligned through dialogue. The landscape approach works on sustainable landscape management while considering the full socio-economic context in an area (IUCN, 2023[22]).

Natural ecosystem: An ecosystem that substantially resembles – in terms of species composition, structure, and ecological function – one that is or would be found in a given area in the absence of major human impacts. This includes human-managed ecosystems where much of the natural species composition, structure, and ecological function are present.

Zero-deforestation: Commodity production, sourcing, or financial investments that do not cause or contribute to deforestation. This definition refers to *gross deforestation*, i.e. any conversion of forests to other land use without regard to compensatory gains in forest cover.

Annex A. Resources

Sources of data on forests and deforestation

Numerous datasets, processing tools, and platforms exist to help gain information on forest area, forest type, deforestation, and reforestation. Datasets refer to either the primary data or the processed data used to produce information. All datasets listed here are freely available to download (e.g. from a website) or view (e.g. in a web data portal). Once downloaded, datasets can be used in more sophisticated analyses using geospatial data processing software.

Processing tools are individual algorithms or software that can be used to add value to data or information to produce higher-order products and analyses. Most tools are freely available, though some require specific licensing for commercial use. Processing platforms are web-based or desktop collections of tools capable of providing end-to-end support for data access and processing. Platforms, as well, can be free to use or require licensing for commercial applications. Collectively, these resources can be very valuable in tracking supply chain impacts at local to global scales.

When seeking and using data on forests, it is important to remember some key points about the information available. Tree cover and forest are different. Tree cover describes a biophysical characteristic of the Earth's surface (e.g. there are trees). Forest, however, is a land use and may, or may not, have tree cover due to management practices (e.g. temporary tree removal from harvest as part of normal management cycles or due to fire). Deforestation, then, refers to a loss of tree cover and a concurrent change in land use from forest to non-forest. Forest degradation refers to a loss of tree cover but no change in land use.

Clearly understanding these terms will help to prioritise datasets based on the information sought.

When looking for information on deforestation in a specific country, a company may wish to reach out to the national focal points for REDD+ or National Forest Monitoring Systems for available public data.

The following tables are not comprehensive and only intended to provide a robust snapshot of available tools and platforms to access forest change related information as of June 2022. Most of the information is synthesised and updated regularly in several lists, such as REDD Compass (https://www.reddcompass.org/) or Open MRV (https://openmrv.org). The reader is invited to consult them for more in-depth understanding of the data and tools.

Table A A.1. Primary datasets

Primary datasets	Info Type	Spatial Resolution	Open Source	Producer	Ease of Use	Update	First data available	Geographic Scale	URL
MODIS mission	Optical Imagery	250-1 000m	Yes	NASA	Moderate	Day	2000	Global	https://modis.gsfc.nasa.gov/
Landsat mission	Optical Imagery	30m	Yes	NASA	Moderate	16-day	1972	Global	https://landsat.gsfc.nasa.gov/
Copernicus mission	Optical and Radar Imagery	10-20m	Yes	ESA	Moderate	5-day	2015	Global	https://www.esa.int/Applications/Observing_the_Earth/Copernicus
Planet NICFI	Optical Imagery	3-5m	Made available through the NICFI programme until at least 2024	Planet	Moderate	Daily	2015	Tropical	https://www.planet.com/nicfi/

Table A A.2. Processed datasets

Processed datasets	Info Type	Spatial Resolution	Open Source	Producer	Ease of Use	Update	First data available	Geographic Scale	URL
UMD GLAD	Imagery, tree cover, change, alerts, fire	30m	Yes	University of Maryland, United States of America	Easy	Month	2000	Global	https://glad.umd.edu/ https://lpdaac.usgs.gov/products/gfcc30fccv001/ https://glad.umd.edu/dataset/gedi https://firms.modaps.eosdis.nasa.gov/map/
JRC TMF	Forest cover change incl. degradation	10-30m	Yes	Joint Research Centre, EU	Easy	Annual	1992	Tropical	https://forobs.jrc.ec.europa.eu/TMF/explorer.php
GLAD alerts (L&S)	Alerts	30m	Yes	University of Maryland, United States of America	Moderate	Month	2017	Global (L), Latin America (S)	https://glad.umd.edu/dataset/glad-forest-alerts
RADD alerts (S)	Alerts	20m	Yes	Wageningen University, the	Moderate	Month	2020	Primary humid tropical forest	http://radd-alert.wur.nl

Processed datasets	Info Type	Spatial Resolution	Open Source	Producer	Ease of Use	Update	First data available	Geographic Scale	URL
				Netherlands					
Dynamic World	LCLU	20m	Yes	Google, World Resources Institute	Moderate	Day	2015	Global	https://developers.google.com/earth-engine/datasets/catalog/GOOGLE_DYNAMICWORLD_V1
ESA CCI	LCLU	300m	Yes	ESA	Moderate	Annual	1992	Global	http://maps.elie.ucl.ac.be/CCI/viewer/index.php
ESA Worldcover	LCLU	10m	Yes	ESA	Easy	Annual	2020	Global	https://worldcover2020.esa.int/viewer
JAXA Forest / Non-forest	Tree cover	25-1 000m	Yes	JAXA	Easy	Annual	2007	Global	https://earth.jaxa.jp/en/data/2555/index.html
JRC TMF	Forest cover change incl. degradation	10-30m	Yes	Joint Research Centre, EU	Easy	Annual	1992	Tropical	https://forobs.jrc.ec.europa.eu/TMF/explorer.php
Crowther Lab layers	Forest restoration potential, biomass, tree density	30m-300m	Yes	ETH Zurich	Easy	-	-	Global	https://crowtherlab.com/maps/#/

Table A A.3. Data access platforms / tools

Data access platforms / tools	Description	URL
Global Forest Watch	Global Forest Watch (GFW 2.0) is an online platform led by WRI that provides data and tools for monitoring forests. GFW 2.0 provides a dashboard with precalculated zonal statistics on various tree cover change and forest extent products, essentially at national and subnational levels. It also allows users to visualise the GLAD datasets in a geoportal and refine those calculations for user-defined zones.	www.globlaforestwatch.org
Terra-i	Terra-i detects land-cover changes resulting from human activities in near real-time, producing updates every 16 days. Currently it works for the whole of Latin America and the tropics. It is led by CIAT.	www.terra-i.org
FAO *Forest Resources Assessment* series	FAO Global Forest Resources Assessment (FRA) provides essential information for understanding the extent of forest resources, their condition, management and uses, at national level.	https://fra-data.fao.org/
OpenForis EarthMap	EarthMap is a tool for quick historical environmental and climate analysis based on Google Earth Engine and developed within FAO's Open Foris Initiative.	https://earthmap.org
MapBiomas	Gathering and releasing LULUCF information in the Pan-Amazon; Brazilian Cerrado, Pampas and Pantanal; El Chaco region; and Indonesian tropical forests.	https://mapbiomas.org

Table A A.4. Data processing platforms / tools

Data processing platforms / tools	Description	URL
Google Earth Engine	Google Earth Engine is a geospatial processing service, powered by Google Cloud Platform. The purpose of Earth Engine is to: provide an interactive platform for geospatial algorithm development at scale; enable high-impact, data-driven science; and make substantive progress on global challenges that involve large geospatial datasets.	https://code.earthengine.google.com/
OpenForis SEPAL	SEPAL is a cloud computing platform that allows users to query and process satellite data quickly and efficiently, tailor their products for local needs, and produce sophisticated and relevant geospatial analyses quickly. Harnessing cloud-based supercomputers and modern geospatial data infrastructures (e.g. Google Earth Engine), SEPAL enables access and processing of a wide range of satellite data.	https://sepal.io
OpenForis Collect Earth	Collect Earth is a tool that enables data collection through Google Earth. In conjunction with Google Earth, Bing Maps and Google Earth Engine, users can analyse high and very high resolution satellite imagery for a wide variety of purposes.	https://openforis.org/tools/collect-earth/
OpenForis Collect Earth Online	Collect Earth Online (CEO) is the next generation of web-based, crowd-sourcing technology for Earth Science analyses. It allows users to collect reference data using high-resolution satellite images and big-data analysis through Google Earth Engine. Multiple users can simultaneously collect information.	https://collect.earth/
Open Data Cubes	The Open Data Cube (ODC) is an Open Source Geospatial Data Management and Analysis Software project that helps harness the power of satellite data. At its core, the ODC is a set of Python libraries and PostgreSQL database that helps users work with geospatial raster data. The ODC provides an open and freely accessible exploitation architecture and seeks to foster a community to develop, sustain, and grow the technology and the breadth and depth of its applications for societal benefit.	https://www.opendatacube.org/
Digital Earth Africa	The DEA platform and services enable African Governments, industry and decision makers to track changes across the continent in unprecedented detail. This provides valuable insights for better decision-making across many areas, including flooding, drought, soil and coastal erosion, agriculture, forest cover, land use and land cover change, water availability and quality, and changes to human settlements.	https://www.digitalearthafrica.org/
EU Forestry Thematic Exploitation Platform	The Forestry Thematic Exploitation Platform (Forestry TEP) enables commercial, governmental and research users in the forestry sector globally to efficiently access satellite data based processing services and tools for generating value-added forest information products. Via the platform, the users can also create and share their own processing services, tools and generated products.	https://f-tep.com/
Proposed EU Observatory	Not yet in operation, the EU Observatory on deforestation and forest degradation is aimed to provide open, transparent and free information related to forest loss, degradation and EU trade in relevant commodities and products.	

Table A A.5. Supply chain mapping tools

Supply chain mapping tools	Description	URL
SPOTT	SPOTT is a free, online platform assessing commodity producers, processors and traders on their public disclosure regarding their organisation, policies, and practices related to environmental, social and governance (ESG) issues. It provides a dashboard to download assessment data, analyse trends, and access further resources.	https://www.spott.org

Supply chain mapping tools	Description	URL
TRASE	Trase is a supply chain mapping tool at scale with three main characteristics: It systematically links individual supply chain actors to specific, subnational production regions, and the sustainability risks and investment opportunities associated with those regions; It identifies the individual companies that export, ship and import a given traded commodity; and It covers all of the exports of a given commodity from a given country of production.	https://supplychains.trase.earth
Open Land Contracts	OpenLandContracts is a global repository of publicly available contracts and related documents for agriculture, forestry, and other land-based investment projects. Users can access original documents in PDF form; the full text of each contract; plain language summaries of contracts' key social, human rights, environmental, fiscal, and operational provisions; and tools to search and compare contracts.	https://openlandcontracts.org

Voluntary sustainability standards and certification systems

Voluntary sustainability standards[6] and certification systems[7] based on them have an important potential role to play in due diligence frameworks covering deforestation, alongside other tools. They often contain very detailed sets of environmental, social and economic criteria which products certified to their standard must meet, together with chain of custody, verification, assurance and monitoring systems for the certification process. Many standard systems have strong participatory and inclusive elements, either because they are organised as multi-stakeholder commodity roundtables or because their standard is regularly reviewed in a participatory process, or both; however, there are significant variations between the different standards and schemes and their governance.

In principle, different types of VSS and certifications can be used as:[8]

- A means of adopting criteria related to the protection of forests and avoiding deforestation after a specific cut-off date for an enterprise's forest policy.
- A source of information in the risk assessment step of a due diligence system.
- A tool to be used in the risk mitigation step of a due diligence system.
- A framework for engaging with and supporting farmers and other actors in the supply chain.

Some VSS and certification systems have developed simpler systems for the verification of a more limited range of criteria when certified materials are mixed with non-certified materials that, for example, are required not to have been harvested illegally. There are also some simpler legality verification schemes, which verify whether products have been produced in accordance with national laws in their countries of origin; these include laws related to deforestation.

VSS and Certification schemes can provide valuable tools to help enterprises implement the steps described in this Handbook, and, importantly, they often also incorporate a wider range of criteria than just forest conservation and land use change. However, companies retain ultimate responsibility for their due diligence and have a responsibility under each Step of the due diligence process. A certification, however strong or comprehensive, cannot replace this responsibility. Instead, companies that use certifications should check and build on the information they receive through their own risk-based checks. Certifications may also not satisfy all the requirements of national due diligence legislation. They should be viewed as an important potential component of, and information source for, the enterprise's due diligence policy, not a substitute for it.

The table below lists some of the main voluntary sustainability standards and certification schemes for commodities mentioned in this Handbook. Only some of those with international coverage are listed; there are also many national and regional schemes, particularly, though not only, for timber and wood products. The table also does not include commodity round tables that have not yet developed certification schemes; examples include the Global Roundtable for Sustainable Beef and the Global Platform for Sustainable Natural Rubber.

There are also government-supported (and sometimes mandated) standards, listed in Table A A.7.

Table A A.6. Voluntary sustainability standards and certification schemes

Standard / certification scheme	Commodities covered	URL
Bonsucro	Sugarcane	https://bonsucro.com
Fairtrade	Wide range of products, including cocoa, coffee, sugar, tea	https://www.fairtrade.net
4C Association (Common Code for the Coffee Community)	Coffee	https://www.4c-services.org

Standard / certification scheme	Commodities covered	URL
International Sustainability and Carbon Certification (ISCC)	Agricultural and forestry biomass, biogenic wastes and residues; mainly used for biofuel feedstocks such as vegetable oils	https://www.iscc-system.org
Forest Stewardship Council (FSC)	Wood products	https://fsc.org
Programme for the Endorsement of Forest Certification (PEFC) (recognises national forest certification systems aligned with PEFC standards)	Wood products	https://pefc.org
ProTerra	Any agricultural commodity; mainly used for soy	https://www.proterrafoundation.org
Rainforest Alliance	Wide range of products, including cocoa, coffee, palm oil, tea	https://www.rainforest-alliance.org
Round Table on Responsible Soy (RTRS)	Corn, soy	https://responsiblesoy.org
Roundtable on Sustainable Biomaterials (RSB)	Wide range of bio-based feedstock and biomass-derived material; mainly used for biofuel feedstocks	https://rsb.org
Roundtable on Sustainable Palm Oil (RSPO)	Palm oil	https://rspo.org
Sustainable Biomass Programme (SBP)	Woody biomass used in large-scale industrial energy production	https://sbp-cert.org

Table A A.7. National sustainability standards and certification schemes

Standard / certification scheme	Commodities covered	URL
African Standard for Sustainable Cocoa	Cocoa	Not available
Indonesian Sustainable Palm Oil (ISPO)	Palm oil	Not available
Malaysian Sustainable Palm Oil	Palm oil	https://www.mpocc.org.my/about-mspo

Other relevant resources

Table A A.8. Other relevant resources

Name	Description	URL
Accountability Framework	Set of norms, definitions, and guidance to achieve ethical supply chains in agriculture and forestry, aiming to bring clarity and consistency in how companies set commitments, take action, and monitor progress toward achieving supply chains free from deforestation, conversion, and human rights violations. Includes protocols and guidelines for many of the steps discussed in this Handbook.	https://accountability-framework.org
CDP Forests	Framework for companies to measure and manage forest-related risks and opportunities, report on progress, and commit to action for the restoration of forests and ecosystems.	https://www.cdp.net/en/forests
'Collective tenure rights for REDD+ implementation and sustainable development'	Technical paper providing information and case studies on the contribution of collective tenure rights to halting deforestation and climate change mitigation (FAO/UN-REDD Programme).	https://doi.org/10.4060/cb3521en
FAO Free, Prior and Informed Consent (FPIC) Manual	Provides information for practitioners about the right to FPIC and how it can be implemented in six steps.	https://www.fao.org/3/i6190e/i6190e.pdf
Global Reporting Initiative (GRI)	Wide range of sustainability reporting standards.	https://www.globalreporting.org
ISEAL	Network of voluntary sustainability standards, including many of those listed above. Sets Codes of Good Practice and Credibility Principles to help users make informed choices over credible standards.	https://www.isealalliance.org
OECD Alignment Assessments process	Seeks to evaluate the alignment of industry or multi-	https://www.oecd.org/corporate/industry-

Name	Description	URL
	stakeholder initiatives, such as certification systems, with the recommendations of OECD Due Diligence Guidance for RBC and the sectoral due diligence guidances.	initiatives-alignment-assessment.htm
OECD e-learning Academy on Responsible Business Conduct	Courses include OECD Due Diligence for Agriculture and Seafood Supply Chains.	https://mneguidelines.oecd.org/oecd-e-learning-academy-on-responsible-business-conduct.htm
Principles for Responsible Investment in Agriculture and Food Systems. Committee on World Food Security.	The Committee on World Food Security (CFS) endorsed the Principles for Responsible Investment in Agriculture and Food Systems on 15 October 2014.They seek to Address the core elements of what makes investment in agriculture and food systems responsible; Identify who the key stakeholders are, and their respective roles and responsibilities with respect to responsible investment in agriculture and food systems; Serve as a framework to guide the actions of all stakeholders engaged in agriculture and food systems by defining Principles which can promote much needed responsible investment, enhance livelihoods, and guard against and mitigate risks to food security and nutrition	https://www.fao.org/3/au866e/au866e.pdf
Voluntary Guidelines *on* the Responsible Governance of Tenure of Land, Fisheries and Forests in the Context of National Food Security (VGGT)	Internationally endorsed Guidelines that serve as a reference and set out principles and internationally accepted standards for the responsible governance of tenure. Accompanied by technical guides, including on respecting free, prior and informed consent, and e-learning courses.	https://www.fao.org/tenure/voluntary-guidelines/en/

References

Accountability Framework (2020), *Definitions*, https://accountability-framework.org/the-framework/contents/definitions/. [4]

CDP/AFI (2022), *From Commitments to Action at Scale*, CDP, https://www.cdp.net/en. [17]

FAO (2022), *FRA 2020 Remote Sensing Survey*, https://www.fao.org/forest-resources-assessment/remote-sensing/fra-2020-remote-sensing-survey/en/. [7]

FAO (2022), *The State of Agricultural Commodity Markets 2022. The geography of food and agricultural trade: Policy approaches for sustainable development*, FAO, https://www.fao.org/documents/card/en/c/cc0471en. [13]

FAO (2021), *First results of Forest Resources Assessment 2020 remote sensing survey*, https://www.fao.org/3/cb7449en/cb7449en.pdf. [8]

FAO (2020), *Global Forest Resources Assessment 2020*, https://www.fao.org/3/ca9825en/ca9825en.pdf. [3]

FAO (2020), *Global Forest Resources Assessment 2020: Terms and Definitions*, https://www.fao.org/3/I8661EN/i8661en.pdf. [21]

FAO (2016), *Free Prior and Informed Consent: An indigenous peoples' right and a good practice for local communities*, http://www.fao.org/3/I6190E/i6190e.pdf. [20]

FAO (2014), *Principles for Responsible Investment in Agriculture and Food Systems (CFS-RAI Principles)*, https://www.fao.org/3/au866e/au866e.pdf. [19]

FAO and UNEP (2020), "The State of the World's Forests 2020", in *The State of the World"s Forests: Forests, Biodiversity and People*, https://www.fao.org/documents/card/en?details=ca8642en. [5]

Federici, S. (2015), "New estimates of CO2 forest emissions and removals: 1990-2015", *Forest Ecology and Management*, Vol. 352, https://doi.org/10.1016/j.foreco.2015.04.022. [6]

Forest Trends (2021), *Illicit Harvest, Complicit Goods: The State of Illegal Deforestation for Agriculture*, https://www.forest-trends.org/wp-content/uploads/2021/05/Illicit-Harvest-Complicit-Goods_rev.pdf. [14]

Geist, H. (2002), "Proximate Causes and Underlying Driving Forces of Tropical Deforestation.", *BioScience*, Vol. 52(2), pp. 143-150, https://doi.org/10.1641/0006-3568(2002)052[0143:PCAUDF]2.0.CO;2. [9]

IUCN (2023), *Landscape Approach*, https://www.iucn.nl/en/our-work/landscape-approach/. [22]

Lacey (2008), *Lacey Act*, https://www.aphis.usda.gov/aphis/ourfocus/planthealth/import-information/lacey-act/lacey-act. [2]

OECD (2018), *OECD Due Diligence Guidance for Responsible Business Conduct*, OECD, http://mneguidelines.oecd.org/OECD-Due-Diligence-Guidance-for-Responsible-Business-Conduct.pdf. [18]

OECD-FAO (2021), *OECD-FAO Agricultural Outlook 2021-2030*, OECD, https://doi.org/10.1787/19428846-en. [10]

OECD-FAO (2016), *OECD-FAO Guidance for Responsible Agricultural Supply Chains*, OECD, https://doi.org/10.1787/9789264251052-en. [1]

Pendrill, F. (2019), "Deforestation displaced: trade in forest-risk commodities and the prospects for a global forest transition", *Environmental Research Letters*, Vol. 14/5, https://doi.org/10.1088/1748-9326/ab0d41. [16]

UN (2019), *World Population Prospects 2019 – Highlights*, https://doi.org/10.18356/13bf5476-en. [11]

UN (n.d.), *Commitment on Eliminating Agricultural Commodity-Driven Deforestation and Increasing Investments in NbS*, https://climatechampions.unfccc.int/system/nature-and-tackling-deforestation/. [23]

Van Dijk, M. (2021), "A meta-analysis of projected global food demand and population at risk of hunger for the period 2010–2050.", *Nature Food*, Vol. 2(7), pp. 494–501, https://doi.org/10.1038/s43016-021-00322-9. [12]

World Bank (2019), *Illegal Logging, Fishing and Wildlife Trade: The costs and how to combat it*, http://hdl.handle.net/10986/32806. [15]

Notes

[1] The OECD FAO Agricultural Outlook 2022-31 illustrates the growing need to promote sustainable agricultural production, including adapting to different region-specific contexts to balance food production with other crops and the conservation of natural resources (OECD-FAO, 2021[10]).

[2] In addition to these global initiatives, many regional and national initiatives exist to combat deforestation in agricultural supply chains.

[3] See for example the Financial Sector Commitment on Eliminating Commodity-driven Deforestation announced at COP26 (UN, n.d.[23]) while at COP 27 countries in the Forest and Climate Leaders' Partnership promised to hold each other accountable for a pledge to end deforestation by 2030. https://www.euronews.com/green/2022/11/07/cop27-more-than-25-countries-band-together-to-keep-deforestation-pledges-made-in-glasgow

[4] See the background note on *Translating a risk-based due diligence approach into law* for further information. http://mneguidelines.oecd.org/translating-a-risk-based-due-diligence-approach-into-law.pdf

[5] Where an audit is deemed appropriate, the independence and quality of audits are critical to their effectiveness. Auditors should be independent, competent and accountable. Enterprises may consider using an independent institution responsible for accrediting auditors, verifying audits, publishing audit reports, implementing modules to build capabilities of suppliers to conduct due diligence, and helping to follow up on grievances of interested parties.

[6] For more information on VSS and their role, see the United Nations Forum on Sustainability Standards (UNFSSS) website: https://unfss.org/home/about-unfss/

[7] Certification is defined by ISEAL as: "The issuance of a third-party statement that fulfilment of specified conformance requirements have been demonstrated (ISEAL, adapted from ISO 17 000)". See https://www.isealalliance.org/sites/default/files/resource/2018-02/ISEAL_Assurance_Code_Version_2.0.pdf

[8] Please see the Background Note on The role of sustainability initiatives in mandatory Due Diligence, for more information: https://mneguidelines.oecd.org/the-role-of-sustainability-initiatives-in-mandatory-due-diligence-note-for-policy makers.pdf

www.ingramcontent.com/pod-product-compliance
Lightning Source LLC
Chambersburg PA
CBHW061224240926
51846CB00006B/1352
* 9 7 8 9 2 6 4 7 2 5 3 2 4 *